NUTSHELLS

Criminal Law

This book is due for return on or before the last date shown below.

NUT**SHELLS**

Criminal Law

TENTH EDITION

by
JOANNE CLOUGH
Solicitor, Senior Lecturer in Law
Northumbria University

ADAM JACKSON
Barrister, Senior Lecturer in Law
Northumbria University

NATALIE WORTLEY
Barrister, Principal Lecturer in Law
Northumbria University

SWEET & MAXWELL

 THOMSON REUTERS

Published in 2014 by Thomson Reuters (Professional) UK Limited
trading as Sweet & Maxwell, Friars House, 160 Blackfriars Road,
London SE1 8EZ
(Registered in England & Wales, Company No 1679046.
Registered Office and address for service:
1 Mark Square, Leonard Street, London, EC2A 4EG

Typeset by YHT Ltd
Printed and bound in Great Britain by CPI Group (UK) Ltd, Croydon, CRO 4YY

*For further information on our products and services, visit
www.sweetandmaxwell.co.uk*

No natural forests were destroyed to make this product;
only farmed timber was used and re-planted.

A CIP catalogue record for this book is available from the British Library.

ISBN 978-0-414-03190-6

Crown copyright material is reproduced with the permission of the Controller of HMSO and
the Queen's Printer for Scotland.

Thomson Reuters and the Thomson Reuters logo are trademarks of Thomson Reuters.
Sweet & Maxwell ® is a registered trademark of Thomson Reuters (Professional) UK
Limited

Contents

Using this book

CHAPTER INTRODUCTIONS open every
chapter, providing an overview
of the topic to be discussed.

The Basis of Interv

INTRODUCTION

The process of judicial review involve
made by bodies exercising public |
~ legality of these decisions ~

.are in all
erendant is involved in a
to win.

CHECKPOINT

Approach adopted to incidents b
sporting events:
- In *Condon v Basi* (CA, 1985), a "|
  local amateur football match w
- In *Watson v British Boxing Boc*
  out that where the plaintiff c'
  boxing ring he does not con
  safety arrangements by t'

CHECKPOINTS
highlight key concepts and define
complex terms, boxed for easy
identification and revision.

KEY CASES present the facts and
judgments in the most influential
case-law, boxed for easy
identification and revision.

~ comp
u secondly, since the
plaintiff cannot be said to cons
time (*Baker v T. E. Hopkins & Soi*

KEY CASE

DANGER INVITES RESCUE; RESCUERS
RESCUE IS TO SAVE LIFE OR LIMB.
Chadwick v British Transport Com
assisted at the scene of a train cr?
as a result of what he saw was he
was in no personal danger (for '
generally see Ch.2).

LEGISLATION HIGHLIGHTERS provide
extracts of the significant legislation,
boxed for easy identification and revision.

> **LEGISLATION HIGHLIGHTER**
>
> Section 149 of the Road Traffic Act (19
> the driver's liability to his passenger
> means that the *volenti* defence is now (
> road traffic accidents.

4. Rescuers
If the defendant's negligence endange
rescue attempt is reasonably forese
~nes v Harwood (CA, 1935))
     ~d is actually the d

COLOUR CODING throughout to
help distinguish cases and legislation
from the narrative. At the first mention,
cases are highlighted in colour and
italicised and legislation is highlighted
in colour and emboldened.

.equent case law has decided ι.
(a) Jews are an ethnic group (*Seide v*
(b) Gypsies are an ethnic group (*CRE v*
(c) Rastafarians are not an ethnic group
    ment [1993] I.R.L.R. 284)
(d) Jehovah's Witnesses are not an ethnic
    Norwich City College case 1502237/97)
(e) RRA covers the Welsh (*Gwynedd CC v*
(f) Both the Scots and the English are cc
    "national origins" but not by "ethn
    Board v Power [1997], *Boyce v Bri*

    ` should be noted that Sikh
         `ra also p

DIAGRAMS AND FLOWCHARTS condense and visually represent detailed information.

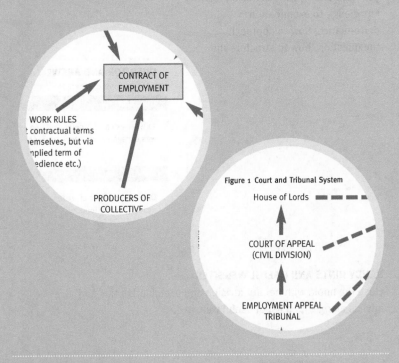

WORK RULES
contractual terms
emselves, but via
nplied term of
edience etc.)

CONTRACT OF
EMPLOYMENT

PRODUCERS OF
COLLECTIVE

Figure 1 Court and Tribunal System

House of Lords

COURT OF APPEAL
(CIVIL DIVISION)

EMPLOYMENT APPEAL
TRIBUNAL

END OF CHAPTER REVISION
CHECKLISTS identify the key take-aways from the chapter.

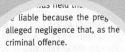

was held the
liable because the pre
alleged negligence that, as the
criminal offence.

REVISION CHECKLIST

You should now understand:

☐ The conditions within which the
and the overlap between the def

☐ *Volenti* is a complete defence ar
because it is more flexible;

END OF CHAPTER QUESTION AND ANSWER SECTION is a chance to practice what you have learnt, with advice on relating knowledge to examination performance, how to approach the question, how to structure the

QUESTION AND ANSWEⱤ

QUESTION

To what extent is a defendant in a
was engaged in an illegal activity af

APPROACH TO THE ANSWER

Outline the effect of *ex tuⱤ*
action can be founde

HANDY HINTS AND USEFUL WEBSITES

close the book, with helpful revision and examination tips and advice, along with a list of useful websites.

HANDY HINTS

Examination questions in employme.
either essay questions or problem ques
format and in what is required of the ex
of question in turn.

Students usually prefer one type
normally opting for the problem ques
examinations are usually set in a wa
least one of each style of question

Very few, if any, questions
Ɽows about a topic, and it
Ɽo make a Ɽ

USEFUL WEBSITES

Official Information
www.parliament.uk—very user-friendly.
www.direct.gov.uk—portal for governm(
www.opsi.gov.uk—Office of Public Sect(
    and statutory instruments available
www.dca.gov.uk—Department for Con
www.dca.gov.uk/peoples-rights/hum
    Unit at the Department for Con
www.homeoffice.gov.uk/police
    the Police and Criminal

Table of Cases

Table of Statutes

Actus reus

INTRODUCTION

A criminal offence is conduct which has been forbidden by the state, such conduct attracting punishment where the law has been breached. All criminal offences, except offences of strict liability (see Ch.3) have two distinct parts which must be proved. These are the actus reus and the mens rea. These terms derive from the Latin phrase "actus non facit reum nisi mens sit rea", i.e. "the act itself does not constitute guilt unless done with a guilty mind". Therefore both a guilty act (actus reus) and a guilty mind (mens rea) must be proven before a criminal offence has been committed. Think of criminal liability like a maths equation. Without all the elements the equation cannot be complete.

The actus reus and mens rea may comprise a number of different matters and these are referred to as the elements of an offence. Thus, for example, in theft the actus reus requires the appropriation of property belonging to another (three elements) while the mens rea requires dishonesty and an intention to permanently deprive (two elements). All elements of both the actus reus and the mens rea must be proven to constitute a criminal offence. This chapter explains the physical part of a criminal offence (actus reus). The mental element (mens rea) is considered in Ch.2.

WHAT IS AN ACTUS REUS?

The actus reus will differ from offence to offence. At the most basic level, the actus reus of an offence will consist of an act or physical element. For example, in the offence of battery, the physical element is the use of unlawful force (see Ch.7). However, very often, more than simply a physical act is required to constitute the actus reus of an offence. For this reason, the actus reus may comprise more than one element. If any element of the actus reus is missing then there is no liability.

Some crimes require the production of consequences as a result of the action (result crimes). For example, in murder the actus reus requires both conduct on the part of the accused (physical element) and death of the victim (consequence). Other crimes require particular circumstances to be present. For example, in the offence of theft, the accused must appropriate property but the property must belong to another, the latter element forming circumstances without which there would be no liability for theft.

As mentioned above, the actus reus alone does not normally amount to a criminal offence. Most offences require a mental element (mens rea) in addition. Therefore in theft, along with the appropriation of property belonging to another (actus reus), the accused must act dishonestly and with an intention to permanently deprive the other of that property (mens rea). Some criminal offences, particularly motoring offences, do not require any mental element. These offences are known as "strict liability" or "absolute liability" offences and will be considered in more detail in Ch.3.

Voluntary conduct

The accused's conduct must be "voluntary" if he is to incur liability (*Bratty v Attorney General of Northern Ireland* (1963)). This means that the action must be a deliberate or willed action on the part of the accused. For example, in *Mitchell* (1983), D pushed another person (E) who in turn lost his balance and knocked into a third person, V. V fell to the ground and fractured his leg. He later died of a pulmonary embolism caused by thrombosis arising from the fracture. While E was the immediate cause of the fracture, his actions were not voluntary. It was D who was charged with and convicted of manslaughter.

Automatism

This is considered in more detail as a defence in Ch.6. Automatism occurs when D performs a physical act or acts but is unaware of what he is doing, or is not in control of his actions. Judges have defined automatism in various ways including "acts performed involuntarily", "unconscious involuntary action", and "involuntary movement of the… limbs of a person". Automatism can be seen as relevant to actus reus in that the act is not a voluntary act, or alternatively in terms of mens rea in that there is no mental element present in relation to the act because the defendant is not aware of what he is doing.

Reflex actions

Sometimes people can respond to something with a spontaneous reflex action over which they have no control. Although slightly different, this is sometimes classed as a form of automatism. The classic example is that given in *Hill v Baxter* (1958) of someone being stung by a swarm of bees while driving, and losing control of the car.

"State of affairs" cases

Some unusual cases cannot be discussed in terms of acts and are often referred to as "state of affairs" cases. These are cases where the actus reus consists of circumstances and sometimes consequences but no "acts", i.e. "being" rather than "doing" offences. In *Winzar v Chief Constable of Kent* (1983), D was convicted of "being found drunk in a highway" contrary to s.12 of the Licensing Act 1872. The police had found D drunk in a hospital and removed him from the premises, subsequently leaving him on a highway in the same state. This conviction was upheld on appeal despite the fact that D was not responsible for being placed on the highway by the officers.

OMISSIONS

> **CHECKPOINT**
>
> "Unless a statute specifically so provides, or ... the common law imposes a duty upon one person to act in a particular way towards another ... a mere omission to act (cannot lead to criminal liability)."
> *Miller* (1983)

Some criminal offences can be committed by omission rather than by a positive act. There are two requirements to be satisfied before liability can be imposed for failing to act:

(1) The crime has to be capable of being committed by omission.

The actus reus of the offence usually makes it clear whether the offence is capable of being committed by omission. For example, in burglary the accused must "enter" a building as a trespasser, thus this requires a positive act. Most of the leading cases relate to offences of murder and manslaughter but offences such as arson, assault, battery and some statutory offences such as failing to provide a specimen of breath, can all be committed by omission.

(2) D must be under a duty to act

The law has recognised a number of situations when D is under a duty to act. The following cases illustrate these situations.

i) Duty arising from a special relationship.

A special relationship between D and the victim can create a duty to act. The courts have recognised relationships between spouses (*Smith* (1979)) and between parent and child (*Gibbins & Proctor* (1918)) as creating such a duty.

ii) Voluntary assumption of responsibility

Someone who voluntarily assumes responsibility for another person also assumes the positive duty to act reasonably for the general welfare of that person and may be liable for omissions which prove fatal.

KEY CASE

GIBBINS & PROCTOR (1918)
Gibbins was the father of a number of children including a seven-year-old child, Nelly. He was living with his girlfriend, Proctor. They kept Nelly separate from the other children and omitted to feed the child so that she died. Gibbins buried Nelly in the brickyard where he worked, claiming that Nelly had left. Both were convicted of murder and their convictions were upheld by the Court of Criminal Appeal on the basis that Gibbins owed a duty of care as her father and Proctor had assumed a duty of care as her carer.

KEY CASE

STONE & DOBINSON (1977)
A couple (S and D) had taken in S's sister to live with them. The sister suffered from anorexia nervosa which deteriorated to the extent that she was confined to bed. The couple omitted to care for her properly, failing to call the doctor or medical services, with the result that the sister died. The couple were held to have assumed a duty of care for the sister and were found guilty of manslaughter.

---

iii) Duty under a contract

A person may be under a positive duty to act because of their obligations under a contract. The duty may be to the other contracting party or to a third person.

PITTWOOD (1902)

D was a railway crossing keeper who forgot to shut the gate before a train came. Someone crossing the line was struck by the train and killed. The court held that D owed a duty to all users of the crossing and not just to his employers. D was accordingly found guilty of manslaughter.

Other examples where contractual duties have been considered to exist are between a hospital anaesthetist and a patient (*Adomako* (1995)) and by a landlord to a tenant (*Singh* (1999)).

iv) Duty due to defendant's prior conduct

If the defendant has acted positively although innocently to create a state of affairs which might cause damage or injury, and subsequently becomes aware of the danger he has created, a duty arises to act reasonably to avert that danger.

MILLER (1983)

D was squatting in a house and fell asleep while smoking. The mattress caught fire and he woke up. Instead of putting out the fire he moved into another room and went back to sleep. The house caught fire and the House of Lords upheld his conviction for arson. D had unwittingly brought about a situation of danger to property. Once he realised this, he was under a self-induced duty to act positively to avert it.

v) Statutory duty of care

In some circumstances a statute makes it a criminal offence to omit to do something. For example, s.170 of the Road Traffic Act 1988 makes it an offence, if one is involved in an accident, to omit to either report it within 24 hours to the police or to give all relevant details to any other person at the scene of the accident reasonably requesting them.

Cessation of duty to act

The issue of when a duty to act ceases can cause difficulties for the courts. In *Airedale NHS Trust v Bland* (1993) the House of Lords attempted to provide guidance on when a person can be released from a duty to act. This was a civil case involving a person in a persistent vegetative state who was on a life support machine following injury in the Hillsborough Stadium disaster. His parents sought to have the life support discontinued. The House of Lords held that it was not unlawful to withdraw artificial nutrition and hydration for such a person. It was lawful not to continue to supply the patient with care which would prolong his life. The House of Lords considered this to be an omission rather than a positive step to end a person's life, as to do the latter would be euthanasia which is illegal in England and Wales.

PROPOSALS FOR REFORM

The Law Commission in its Report No. 218 *Offences Against the Person and General Principles* (1994), in relation to offences against the person, states that liability for omission should be limited to serious offences, namely homicide, intentional serious injury, torture, unlawful detention, kidnapping, abduction and aggravated abduction. The Law Commission also decided for the present not to try to limit the common law duties to act which currently give rise to liability for omissions. Some academics suggest that there should be a positive duty to act where a person could save someone's life without putting themselves in danger. This suggestion is not without its difficulties. For example, who would be prosecuted in a situation where there was a crowd of people who failed to rescue a drowning child?

CAUSATION

In "result crimes" (i.e. where a consequence is part of the actus reus), it is necessary to prove that the accused's conduct caused the required consequence. Murder is a clear example of a result crime as death is a consequence required as part of the actus reus. It is for the jury to decide if the accused caused the prohibited result following prohibited conduct.

There are two key tests which must both be satisfied to establish causation:

(1) Causation in fact
This is established by applying the "but for" test, which requires proof that the consequence would not have occurred "but for" the accused's actions.

D poisoned his mother's drink with intent to kill her. She died after taking some of the drink but medical evidence found that the cause of death was a heart attack rather than poisoning. D was charged with murder but acquitted as he had not caused his mother's death in fact (note that he was convicted of attempted murder).

(2) Causation in law

This principle is concerned with whether the prohibited consequence is the fault of the accused. There must be a complete chain of causation between the accused's action and the consequence to establish causation in law. The de minimis principle states that where D's act is a minimal contribution to the consequence, D will not be the legal cause of death. It has been established in *Pagett* (1983) that for liability to exist, D's conduct need not be the sole or even the main cause of death but it must contribute significantly to the result. In *Hughes* (2013) the court considered that a cause was "significant" if it was "more than minimal". Where there are multiple causes more than one person can be held responsible for the result.

Intervening acts

Sometimes, after the accused's initial act, and before the required consequence occurs, there is an intervening act or event which contributes to that consequence. If the intervening act or event is completely unconnected with the defendant's act, was unforeseeable, and brought about the consequence on its own, then it breaks the chain of causation and the defendant incurs no liability for the consequence. If the consequence is caused by a combination of the two causes and the defendant's act remains a significant cause, then the defendant will still be liable.

Actions of third parties

Where a third party does something between the accused's act/omission and the result, this may break the chain of causation.

D was hiding in his girlfriend's flat when police were trying to arrest him for various offences. D armed himself with a shotgun and used his girlfriend's body as a shield, putting her between himself and the police. D fired at officers and they returned fire, three bullets hitting the girlfriend. She died from the wounds. D was convicted of man-slaughter. He appealed on the basis that the death was caused by the police officers. His appeal was dismissed. Where the third party act is a reasonable response to D's initial act, the chain will not be broken.

Occasionally, the victim will react to the accused's actions and con-tribute to the result. It has been held that where the victim contributes to the consequence, the chain of causation will only be broken if the victim's act is so "daft" or unexpected that no reasonable person could be expected to foresee it.

KEY CASE

ROBERTS (1972)

A car driver gave a lift to a young woman. He ordered her to remove her clothes and began pulling at her coat. She opened the door and jumped out of the moving car, suffering some injuries. He appealed against his conviction for assault occasioning actual bodily harm, claiming that he had not caused her injuries. Dismissing the appeal, the Court of Appeal held that where a victim is injured in attempting to escape from threatened violence, the test of causation is whether the injuries were "the natural result of what the [accused] said and did, in the sense that [they] could reasonably have been foreseen as the consequence of what he was saying or doing".

A refusal by the victim to accept treatment is not an intervening act and it will not break the chain of causation. In *Dear* (1996), D had slashed V several times with a knife, causing a severed artery. V died from blood loss a few days later and D was charged with murder. At the trial, D claimed that the chain of causation had been broken by V, who had committed suicide by either re-opening the wounds or failing to treat re-opened wounds. The jury convicted D on the basis that the wounds remained an "operating" and "substantial" cause of death.

The thin skull rule

CHECKPOINT

"It has long been the policy of the law that those who use violence on other people must take their victim as they find them. This in our judgement means the whole man, not just the physical man." Lawton L.J. in *Blaue* (1975).

Due to this rule, the accused does not escape liability if his victim is susceptible to injury or has a belief that prevents the victim from accepting treatment. In *Blaue* (1976), D stabbed his victim, piercing her lung. She refused on religious grounds to accept a blood transfusion which would have saved her life. The Court of Appeal held that her refusal of treatment, whether reasonable or unreasonable, did not break the chain of causation. It was said that the accused must "take his victim as he finds her", i.e. in this case, a Jehovah's Witness who refused treatment.

It can be argued that the same approach should also apply to an intervening act by the victim. An act by the victim which is so "daft" as to be totally unforeseeable can, if it alone brings about the consequence, break the chain of causation (see *Roberts*, above).

Medical negligence cases

The courts have had to consider a number of murder/manslaughter cases in which the acts of the victim's medical team have contributed to the victim's death. The courts are now very unwilling, as a matter of policy, to find that medical treatment has broken the chain of causation when the treatment follows an initial unlawful act by someone else. The first two cases below conflict with each other. The first case has subsequently been distinguished on its own particular facts and has very little general application any longer.

KEY CASE

JORDAN (1956)
D stabbed his victim, who died several days later after undergoing medical treatment. It was finally established on appeal that the wound had been healing well but the medical treatment was grossly negligent. The victim had unnecessarily been given an antibiotic to which he was allergic. This "palpably wrong" treatment may have been the medical cause of death. The court held that the jury might have reached a verdict of not guilty if they had had all the medical evidence, and the conviction was quashed.

KEY CASE

SMITH (1959)
D, a soldier, stabbed another soldier, who was carried to the medical officer in charge. The medical officer was dealing with a series of emergencies and failed to appreciate the seriousness of the victim's wounds. The treatment he gave him was not beneficial and may well

have made his condition worse. The victim died of his stab wounds. D was found guilty of murder and appealed. Dismissing the appeal, and distinguishing Jordan, the court held that D's stabbing was an operating and substantial cause of death. The chain of causation will be broken only if the original wound is merely the setting in which another cause operates, i.e. only if the second cause is so overwhelming as to make the original wound merely part of the history.

The Court of Appeal has subsequently confirmed the approach taken in *Smith*, indicating that *Jordan* has virtually no relevance any more, except in the most "extraordinary or extreme" case.

KEY CASE

CHESHIRE (1991)

D shot his victim. Taken to hospital, the victim contracted a respiratory infection causing a respiratory blockage. He died from the operation which was consequently undertaken, and he was possibly negligently treated by the doctors. Dismissing D's appeal against his murder conviction, the Court of Appeal held that even where negligent treatment is the immediate cause of death, that does not break the chain of causation unless it was so independent of the accused's acts and so potent in causing the death, as to render the acts of the accused insignificant.

Where doctors cease treatment in a situation where there is no prospect of the victim recovering, this will not break the chain of causation even where this medical intervention is the final cause of death. In *Malcherek* (1981), D's victim was put on a life support machine as a result of the injuries D inflicted. After several days, and acting in accordance with the practice of a received body of medical opinion, doctors turned off the machine and the victim died. D was convicted of murder and appealed on the issue of causation, which he said should have been put to the jury. The appeal was dismissed. The court said that D's act was a substantial cause of death and any other contributory cause was immaterial.

PROPOSALS FOR REFORM

In 2002, the Law Commission produced a working paper with a proposal to codify the law on causation. It was suggested that a defendant would be considered to have caused a result which is an element of an offence when,

(a) he does an act which makes a substantial and operative contribution to its occurrence or, (b) he omits to do an act which he is under a duty to do according to the law relating to the offence, and, the failure to act makes a substantial and operative contribution to its occurrence. To date the common law position on which these proposals are based, still prevails.

REVISION CHECKLIST

You should now know and understand:

- [ ] that a criminal offence requires both actus reus and mens rea;
- [ ] that the actus reus refers to the physical element of the crime; this can comprise conduct, consequences and/or circumstances depending on the offence;
- [ ] that some offences can be committed by failing to act;
- [ ] the courts have identified circumstances in which a duty to act is imposed;
- [ ] in result crimes, there must be a causal link between the accused's conduct and the consequence/result;
- [ ] the principles of causation—there must be factual causation and legal causation.

QUESTION AND ANSWER

QUESTION

Tim has been charged with manslaughter. He was involved in a fight when he punched James, who fell and hit his head on the edge of the pavement. While James was unconscious, a bystander called the paramedics. They arrived ten minutes later and dropped James while they were putting him into the ambulance van. This aggravated the internal head injuries caused by James hitting his head on the pavement and James required surgery. The anaesthetist was a young doctor who gave James too much anaesthetic, which put James into a coma. After a few days the medical team declared that there was no hope of James recovering and they switched off his life support machine.

Explain, with authority, whether there are any intervening acts in this scenario which might break the chain of causation.

You should start by looking for anything in the facts that might constitute a break in the chain of causation. This might be the act of a third party, the act of a medical professional or the act of the victim, for example. Then take each in turn, applying the law on causation to each incident separately, to determine whether each incident has caused a break in the chain of causation.

Answer guide:

James hitting his head on the pavement. This occurred as a direct result of D's actions and does not break the chain of causation.

Paramedics dropping James. This does not break the chain of causation under the principles in *Smith*. The original injury remains the operating cause of death.

Young anaesthetist. This is similar to the events in *Cheshire* where the chain of causation was not broken. The original injury remained the substantial and operating cause and the treatment was neither independent nor potent enough in itself for it to break the chain of causation. Note that if the doctor is considered to be a cause of death, it is possible to prosecute him/her also for their role in the death.

Switching off life support. Where doctors cease treatment in circumstances where there is no prospect of recovery, this does not break the chain of causation under the principles in *Malcherek*.

Mens rea

INTRODUCTION

As outlined in Ch.1, many offences require a physical element, the actus reus, and a mental element, the mens rea. This chapter is concerned with the latter.

Mens rea is the culpable state of mind which is necessary, together with the actus reus, for a criminal offence to be committed. The mens rea required varies from crime to crime. There are a number of states of mind which, separately or together, can constitute the necessary mens rea for a criminal offence.

INTENTION

Intention must be distinguished from motive, which is irrelevant to liability. A motive might help to prove intent but it is not the same thing as intent. Where a criminal offence requires intent as its mens rea, this generally requires proof that the accused *desired* a particular result. There are two types of intent in criminal law as outlined below:

Direct intent
Direct intent is where the consequence is desired and the accused decides to bring it about, or to do his best to do so. For example, for murder, the accused must intend to kill or cause serious harm to the victim. Thus, D will have direct intent if he desires that the victim either dies or suffers serious injury as a result of his actions.

Oblique intent
Oblique intent (also referred to as indirect intent) is where the accused does not desire a particular consequence but realises that the consequence is *virtually certain* to occur as a result of his actions. This is not intention in itself. However, if the accused foresaw the consequence as virtually certain, that may lead the jury to conclude that the accused did intend to produce the consequence.

The degree of foresight required for oblique intent has been an ongoing issue for the courts over the years. The starting point was *DPP v Smith* (1961), in which the House of Lords stated that there was an irrebutable presumption that an accused foresaw and intended any "natural consequence" of his actions and that the test for determining what was a natural consequence was a purely objective one (i.e. what an outsider would consider to be a natural consequence of the accused's actions). This was reversed by the Criminal Justice Act 1967 s.8, which states that in determining whether a person has committed an offence, a court or jury shall not be bound to infer that a result was intended or foreseen only where it is a "natural and probable" consequence of those actions. Two cases followed shortly after, discussing the same point:

KEY CASE

MOLONEY (1985)

D and his stepfather had a shooting contest to see who could load and fire a shotgun faster. D loaded and aimed his gun first. It was aimed at his stepfather who challenged him to fire. D did this and killed his stepfather. He was charged with murder. The direction to the jury on intention was that D had the necessary mens rea if he had foreseen death as a "probable consequence" of his actions, even if he did not desire it. The House of Lords quashed D's murder conviction, substituting a verdict of guilty of manslaughter. It was held that only an intention to kill or to cause really serious injury would suffice for murder. Lord Bridge suggested guidelines which could be given to a jury to help them decide upon the issue of intention: (1) Was death or really serious injury a natural consequence of what the accused did? (2) Did the accused realise that death or really serious injury was a natural consequence of what the accused did? If the jury considered that the answer to both of these questions was yes, that was not conclusive proof of intention but was something from which the jury might infer that the accused intended death or really serious injury.

KEY CASE

HANCOCK AND SHANKLAND (1986)

D and another had dropped concrete blocks onto a motorway from a bridge in order to block the road and stop a taxi which was carrying a working miner to work during a miners' strike. One block hit the taxi's windscreen and killed the driver. At the murder trial, the judge directed the jury using the guidelines given by Lord Bridge in *Moloney* (above).

The House of Lords quashed the resulting convictions for murder and substituted manslaughter convictions. Their Lordships held that the *Moloney* guidelines were defective since they did not direct the jury to consider the matter of probability. The jury should be asked to consider: (1) Was death or really serious injury a natural and probable consequence of what the accused did? (2) Did the accused realise that death or really serious injury was a natural and probable consequence of what the accused did? The jury should be told that the more probable it was, the more likely it was that the accused foresaw it; and the more probable the accused realised it to be, the more likely it was that he intended it. These were guidelines which the jury could be given to help them to decide whether to draw the inference that the accused intended death or really serious injury.

Following these cases, the law was clarified by the Court of Appeal in *Nedrick* (1986).

KEY CASE

NEDRICK (1986)

D pushed lighted material through a letter box in order to frighten his victim, but in fact killed two occupants of the house. The judge directed the jury that if D realised that death was "highly likely" to result, then he was guilty of murder. The Court of Appeal allowed D's appeal, holding that the judge had equated foresight with intention. The judge should have made it clear that it was for the jury to decide whether D had the necessary intention. Lord Lane C.J. gave a model direction which increased the degree of foresight required and set a clear precedent for the law on oblique intent:

"... the jury should be directed that they are not entitled to infer the necessary intention unless they feel sure that death or serious bodily harm was a *virtual certainty* (barring some unforeseen intervention) as a result of the defendant's actions and that the defendant appreciated that such was the case".

The leading case is now that of *Woollin* (1999). In this case, the House of Lords retained the high degree of foresight (virtual certainty) but amended the word "infer" to the word "find", stating that the latter would be more easily understood by juries.

KEY CASE

WOOLLIN (1999)

D lost his temper and threw his three-month-old son on to a hard surface, thereby killing him. At D's trial for murder the judge directed the jury in accordance with the model direction given by Lord Lane C.J. in *Nedrick*. He went on, however, to say that the jury could infer the necessary intent if they were satisfied that D realised and appreciated that there was a substantial risk that he would cause serious injury. Quashing the murder conviction and substituting a conviction for manslaughter, the House of Lords held that the latter part of the direction was wrong. Their Lordships specifically upheld the correctness of the model direction suggested by Lord Lane in *Nedrick* (see above), saying that it may be appropriate to give such a direction in any case where the defendant may not have desired the result of his act. Their Lordships did suggest, however, that the word "infer" in that model direction be changed to "find" and made it clear that the guidelines given in *Hancock and Shankland* are no part of the model direction.

The model direction in *Nedrick* (as amended by their Lordships in *Woollin*) is not a definition of intention. It is merely guidance to assist a jury in establishing whether the defendant had the necessary intention (*Matthews and Alleyne* (2003)). Thus, if the jury finds that the defendant appreciated that death was a virtual certainty (in a murder trial), that finding allows, but does not require, the jury to conclude that he intended death. The jury must be left in no doubt that this issue is for them alone to consider and decide upon. This model direction is probably relevant to all offences requiring proof of intention and not just murder, although in *Woollin*, Lord Steyn said that intention did not necessarily have the same meaning throughout the criminal law.

Overlap with recklessness?

There is a distinction between oblique intent and recklessness (see below). If the accused foresees a consequence as *likely*, *probable*, or even just *possible*, and he goes ahead with his action and the consequence does indeed result, the accused can be said to have caused it recklessly.

Specific and basic intent

The distinction between crimes of basic intent and crimes of specific intent is important principally in relation to a defence based on voluntary intoxication. This is considered in Ch.6.

RECKLESSNESS

Recklessness is the taking of an unjustified risk. This is sufficient for many crimes such as assault, battery and criminal damage. The courts have been troubled with whether recklessness should be tested objectively or subjectively and the decisions have come full circle as the following cases illustrate.

Cunningham recklessness

The original test for recklessness arose from the case of *Cunningham* (1957) and was said to be a subjective one, i.e. the defendant must himself have realised the risk.

KEY CASE

CUNNINGHAM (1957)
D was charged under s.23 of the Offences against the Person Act 1861 with "maliciously administering a noxious thing so as to endanger life". He broke a gas meter to steal the money in it and the gas seeped out and into a neighbouring house where the victim lived. This made her ill, endangering her life. Quashing his conviction, the Court of Appeal held that the word "maliciously" did not require any wickedness but did require either intention or recklessness, the latter requiring that the accused had himself foreseen the possibility of the consequence occurring (here, that the noxious substance, gas, might be inhaled and thereby endanger life).

This definition was used when the courts were dealing with the issue of whether an accused was "malicious" for the purposes of the Offences Against the Person Act 1861. When the term "recklessness" started to appear as the mens rea for various offences (for example in the Criminal Damage Act 1971), there was no statutory definition provided. Thus, the courts continued to use the subjective test.

Caldwell recklessness

A much wider and largely objective test for recklessness was introduced in *Caldwell* (1982). It covered the situation where the risk of the consequence occurring would have been obvious to an "ordinary, prudent individual" even though the accused gave no thought to the possibility.

MENS REA

17

KEY CASE

CALDWELL (1982)

D deliberately started a fire at his victim's hotel. He was charged with intentionally or recklessly damaging property belonging to another, being reckless as to whether the life of another would be endangered thereby. He claimed that he had not realised that there was anyone in the hotel and had not realised that life would be endangered. The House of Lords held that a person was reckless as to a consequence if two requirements were satisfied: (1) the accused's actions created a risk of that consequence and the risk would be obvious to an ordinary prudent sober person and (2) the accused either failed to give any thought to that possibility, or recognised the risk and nevertheless went ahead with his actions. According to their Lordships, this definition of recklessness applied to any modern statutory offence which included the word "reckless", "recklessness" or "recklessly".

Goodbye to *Caldwell*

In the years following the decision in *Caldwell,* the courts had to decide which offences were subject to the definition of recklessness in *Cunningham* and which were subject to the *Caldwell* definition. It was held that the *Cunningham* definition applied to offences against the person: *Savage, Parmenter* (1991). It also became clear that *Caldwell* recklessness had no place in involuntary manslaughter by gross negligence: *Adomako* (1994) (see Ch.9). Nor did it have any place in the law of rape: *Satnam* (1984). *Caldwell* recklessness did apply to the statutory offences of reckless driving and causing death by reckless driving: *Lawrence* (1981) and *Reid* (1992). The **Road Traffic Act 1991**, however, replaced those two offences with the offences of dangerous driving and causing death by dangerous driving. Thus, by 2003 the *Caldwell* definition of recklessness had come to apply to only a small range of offences, probably restricted to offences of criminal damage in the **Criminal Damage Act 1971** and to offences of reckless driving committed before July 1992. In 2003, *Caldwell* became completely redundant, when it was reversed by the House of Lords in *G and Another* (2003).

KEY CASE

G & ANOTHER (2003)

Two boys, aged 11 and 13, entered the back yard of a shop, put newspapers beneath wheelie bins there, and set light to the newspapers. The fire spread to the wheelie bins and then to the shop and other commercial premises, causing about £1 million worth of damage.

Neither boy realised that there was any risk that the fire might spread to the buildings. They were charged under the **Criminal Damage Act 1971** with recklessly damaging property belonging to another, namely the buildings. Quashing their conviction, the House of Lords held that the decision in *Caldwell* had been wrong and should be departed from. By using the word "recklessly" rather than the word "maliciously" in the **Criminal Damage Act**, Parliament had not intended a different meaning but was simply using a modern word. The subjective test was reinstated and remains good law today.

In *G and Another*, Lord Bingham set out the current subjective test for recklessness.

That definition was taken from the Draft Criminal Code Bill annexed to the Law Commission's report entitled *A Criminal Code for England and Wales* (1989, Law Com No. 177).

The decision in *G and Another* was limited to the meaning of recklessness in the **Criminal Damage Act 1971**. However, by the time of *G and Another*, it appears that *Caldwell* recklessness did not have a wider application in any event. Thus *Caldwell* is now a matter of history. *G and Another* has restored *Cunningham* recklessness.

NEGLIGENCE

Negligence consists of a falling below the standard of the ordinary reasonable man, and either doing something he would not do, or not doing something which he would do. The test is objective, based on the hypothetical person. Not all negligent behaviour is criminal. Relatively few crimes are defined in terms of negligence. The main one, a form of manslaughter, requires gross negligence (see *Adomako* in Ch.9). For examples of some other crimes of negligence, see harassment (Ch.7) and causing or allowing the death of a child or vulnerable adult (Ch.9).

DISHONESTY

This form of mens rea is used exclusively in the Theft Act 1968 and the Fraud Act 2006 (see Chs 10 and 11). There is no statutory definition for the term but the leading case is *Ghosh* (1982) where a combined subjective and objective approach to establishing dishonesty is adopted. See Ch.10 for details.

TRANSFERRED MALICE

The defendant will be liable for an offence if he has the necessary mens rea and commits the actus reus even if the victim differs from the one intended, or the consequence occurs in a different way to that intended. Thus an intention to cause a particular kind of harm to X can be used to justify a conviction of causing that same kind of harm to Y. This is the principle of transferred malice.

KEY CASE

LATIMER (1886)
D aimed a blow at one person with his belt. The belt recoiled off that person and hit the victim, who was severely injured. The court held that D was liable for maliciously wounding the victim. His malice, i.e. his mens rea, was transferred from his intended to his unintended victim.

One limitation to the doctrine of transferred malice, however, is where D, with the mens rea of one crime, commits the actus reus of a different crime. In this situation, he cannot be convicted of either offence as there must be compatibility between the crime intended and the crime charged. This is demonstrated in the case of *Pembliton* (1874) below.

KEY CASE

PEMBLITON (1874)
D threw a stone at some people. He missed, and broke a window. He was not guilty of damaging the window as he had no mens rea for that offence and the mens rea for a completely different offence could not be transferred to make him liable.

COINCIDENCE OF ACTUS REUS AND MENS REA

One final problem in this area concerns the coincidence in time of the actus reus and the mens rea. The two must coincide for there to be criminal liability. The courts have developed ways of finding coincidence of actus reus and mens rea when the events take place over a period of time and constitute a course of events.

Continuing acts

One way is to say that an actus reus is sometimes a continuing act. Thus, when the mens rea is formed at a later time, it can effectively coincide with the ongoing actus reus.

FAGAN V METROPOLITAN POLICE COMMISSIONER (1969)
D accidentally drove his car on to a policeman's foot. When D realised what he had done, he refused to remove it immediately. The court held that the actus reus of the assault was a continuing act in progress throughout the time the car was on the policeman's foot. Therefore the subsequent mens rea could, and did, coincide with the actus reus at a later stage. D was found guilty of assault.

One transaction

The second way the courts have dealt with the problem is to consider a continuing series of acts to be "one transaction" for the purposes of the criminal law. If actus reus and mens rea are both present at some time during this transaction, then there is liability.

THABO MELI AND OTHERS (1954)
The Ds had attempted to kill their victim by beating him over the head. Thinking him dead, they threw the body over a cliff. He died from the fall and exposure, and not from the beating. The Privy Council held that this was all one series of acts carrying out a preconceived plan of action. They could not be viewed as separate acts. Actus reus and mens rea were each present during different parts of the transaction, and the Ds were therefore guilty of murder.

This approach has subsequently been followed in a number of cases. In *Church* (1966), the same reasoning was applied where there was no preconceived plan and D, mistakenly thinking he had killed the victim, disposed of the "body" in a canal thereby causing death. His manslaughter conviction was upheld on appeal. Similarly, in *Le Brun* (1991), D committed an initial assault on his wife by punching her so that she became unconscious. In trying to remove what he believed to be her corpse so as to cover up his crime, he unintentionally killed her as a result of a blow to the head. The Court of Appeal confirmed and applied the reasoning in *Church* and D was convicted of manslaughter. This kind of reasoning is a way to avoid an unjust result.

PROPOSALS FOR REFORM

The Law Commission Report *Offences Against the Person and General Principles*, No.218 (1994) is the most recent statement of recommended reforms in the area of mens rea. Intention is defined in the report as including knowledge that a result will occur in the ordinary course of events if D were to succeed in his purpose of causing some other result. The report's definition of recklessness has effectively been incorporated into the law by the decision in *G and Another* (see above). It is unlikely that there will be any further reform in this area.

REVISION CHECKLIST

You should now know and understand:

- [ ] mens rea is the mental element in a criminal offence;
- [ ] the actus reus and mens rea of an offence must coincide for D to incur liability;
- [ ] each crime has a different mens rea contained in the definition of the offence;
- [ ] types of mens rea include intention, recklessness, dishonesty and negligence;
- [ ] intention can be either direct or oblique;
- [ ] the test for recklessness is a subjective one, based on what the accused foresaw as a risk of a consequence occurring.

QUESTION AND ANSWER

QUESTION

Even after the House of Lords decision in *Woollin* (1999), the meaning of intention is not entirely clear. Discuss.

ADVICE AND THE ANSWER

This essay is asking you to consider the legal issue of intention. It is asking you to consider the meaning of intention as outlined in the case of *Woollin* and to discuss whether, in light of this judgment, the meaning of intention is clear or not.

Suggested essay plan:

Introduction:

- Explain the concept of intention—mens rea required for the most serious of crimes. A subjective test (what was in D's mind).
- Explain both types of intention: direct intent (aim/purpose/desire of D) and indirect/oblique intent (did D foresee consequence as a virtually certain result of his actions? If yes, this is *evidence* of direct intent).
- Essay concerns indirect/oblique intent as this was what the decision in *Woollin* dealt with.

Explain law leading up to Woollin

- Leading authority in 1960 was *DPP v Smith*—objective test was "not what the Defendant contemplated but what the ordinary reasonable man or woman would in all the circumstances of the case have contemplated as the natural and probable result".
- Overruled by **Criminal Justice Act 1967** s.8—A court or jury shall consider all the evidence to decide whether D foresaw or intended a particular result and shall not be bound to infer that D intended or foresaw a result of his actions simply because it was a natural and probable consequence of those actions. Therefore, where a result will certainly occur as a result of the defendant's actions, it will be easy for the jury to infer intention. Where a result is extremely unlikely to occur as a result of the defendant's actions, it would be very harsh for the jury to decide that the defendant intended that result.

MENS REA

23

- *Hyam v DPP* (1975): High probability that the consequence would occur was sufficient to prove intention. The Court did not overrule the decision in *Smith* but felt that the **Criminal Justice Act 1967** had already made a change in the law.
- *Moloney* (1985): Golden rule is to let the jury's good sense decide whether the defendant acted with the necessary intent. Referred to natural consequence of an action as being sufficient to establish foresight. Low threshold—"natural" is not the same as "probable" for example.
- *Hancock* (1986): Added to the *Moloney* guidelines explaining that the greater the probability of the consequence, the more likely that the defendant foresaw that consequence, therefore the greater the probability that the consequence was intended.
- Looking at probability as an indicator of intention-*Nedrick* (1986): The jury should be directed that they are not entitled to infer the necessary intention unless they feel sure that the consequence was a virtual certainty (barring some unforeseen intervention) as a result of the defendant's actions and that the defendant appreciated that was the case. Higher threshold than where the outcome was "probable".
- *Woollin* (1999) upheld the point in *Nedrick* but amended the word "infer" to the word "find". Purpose was to ensure clarity of expression.

Evaluate the question:
- Discuss clarity of the word "find". If the evidence before the jury suggests that the consequence was a "virtual certainty" then the jury may go on to "find" that he intended that consequence. May suggest that there is a further stage that the jury must go through before reaching the conclusion that the Defendant intended the action.
- Discuss removing requirement to "find" intention. Perhaps it would be clearer if the jury was simply left with the proposition that if the consequence was a virtual certainty of the defendant's actions and the defendant realised this, then intent is quite simply proven. However, would this be too similar to the test for recklessness? In *Matthews & Alleyne* (2003) (the defendants pushed the victim off a bridge into water knowing that he couldn't swim) the court queried this. If the jury was sure that the appellants appreciated the certainty of the victim's death, then it is impossible to see how the jury could not have found that the appellants intended the victim to die.
- Discuss whether intention should mean direct intention only. This

would alleviate the issues raised by *Woollin*. Discuss overlap between indirect intention and recklessness.
- Discuss Law Commission proposals for statutory definition of intention.

Conclusion

Form overall conclusion to question posed.

Strict liability

INTRODUCTION

There are some crimes for which, with regard to at least one element of the actus reus (e.g. a particular circumstance or required consequence), no mens rea is required. The defendant need not have intended or known about that circumstance or consequence. These are strict liability offences.

Strict liability offences require proof of the actus reus of the offence and proof that the accused's actions were voluntary. The accused cannot claim that he took all reasonable steps to avoid committing the offence (defence of due diligence), nor can he claim that he made a mistake as to the facts (defence of mistake) in order to avoid conviction for a strict liability offence.

It is untrue to say that crimes of strict liability never require mens rea. Mens rea may well be required with regard to one particular element of the actus reus. For example, in the case of *Prince* (1875) D was charged with taking an unmarried girl under the age of 16 years out of the possession of her father against his will, contrary to s.55 of the **Offences Against the Person Act 1861**. D knew that the girl he deliberately took was in the possession of her father but believed her to be 18 years old. He was convicted as he had the intention to remove her from her father's possession. Mens rea was required for this part of the actus reus (intention) however the court held that it was not necessary that D knew the girl's age. This part of the actus reus was considered to be strict liability.

Occasionally no mens rea is required at all. Such offences are known as crimes of "absolute liability" and do not require proof that the accused's actions are voluntary. An example of an absolute liability offence can be found in *Winzar v Chief Constable of Kent* (1983) discussed in Ch.1.

WHAT SORT OF OFFENCES ARE STRICT LIABILITY OFFENCES?

There are very few common law strict liability offences. Those that still exist are public nuisance, contempt of court and outraging public decency. Nearly all strict liability offences are created by statute and they are generally regulatory in nature.

DETERMINING WHETHER AN OFFENCE IS STRICT LIABILITY

It is not always easy from the definition of an offence to determine whether it is one of strict liability. The courts start with the presumption that mens rea is an essential ingredient in any offence.

KEY CASE

SWEET V PARSLEY (1969)
D was a landlady of a farmhouse who did not live on the premises but visited occasionally. Her lodgers smoked cannabis, although she was unaware of this. She was charged with being concerned in the management of premises which were used for the purposes of smoking cannabis contrary to s.5 of the (now repealed) **Dangerous Drugs Act 1965**. The magistrates and the Divisional Court held that no mens rea was necessary for this element of the actus reus and found her guilty. The House of Lords on further appeal quashed the conviction and said that this was not an offence of strict liability. Lord Reid re-stated the general principle that where a statute says nothing about mens rea, there is a presumption that mens rea will be required. If Parliament wishes to create a crime of strict liability then it must make its intention manifest. In this case there would be no point in imposing strict liability since no degree of vigilance by the owner of the premises could prevent tenants smoking cannabis. His Lordship also made the basic distinction between crimes which were truly criminal, where penalties were severe and mens rea should be required, and purely regulatory offences with minor penalties. Such offences were "quasi-criminal" and strict liability was a practical and acceptable way of dealing with them.

This explains one kind of strict liability offence but not the "protection of the public" type of offence. This explanation should be compared with the later one in *Gammon (Hong Kong) Ltd v Attorney-General of Hong Kong* (1984) (see below).

The *Gammon* criteria

Following on from this was the case of *Gammon (Hong Kong) Ltd v Attorney General of Hong Kong* (1984) in which the court laid down criteria to assist in determining whether an offence was one of strict liability. They retained the presumption in favour of mens rea for every offence but outlined situations when the presumption could be rebutted.

KEY CASE

GAMMON (HONG KONG) LTD v ATTORNEY GENERAL OF HONG KONG (1984)
This Privy Council case involved D deviating from building plans in a material way, contrary to the Hong Kong Building Ordinances. The Court had to decide whether it was necessary to prove that D knew the deviation was material or whether this was a strict liability matter. The Privy Council set out a list of factors to be considered in identifying a strict liability offence. In summary:

1. There is a presumption that mens rea is required for every statutory offence.
2. The presumption can be displaced by clear wording in a statute or by necessary implication from the effect of the statute.
3. The presumption is particularly strong where the offence is "truly criminal".
4. The only situation in which the presumption can be displaced is where the statute is concerned with an issue of social concern such as public safety.
5. Even where the statute is concerned with such an issue, the presumption stands unless it can be shown that the creation of strict liability will be effective to promote the objects of the statute by encouraging greater vigilance to prevent the commission of the prohibited act.

Thus the courts will start with a presumption in favour of mens rea but may look to the wording of the Act to determine whether the offence is one of strict liability. Words such as "knowingly", "recklessly", "permitting" or "intentionally" will indicate an element of mens rea. If the particular section charged is silent on the matter, the Court will look to the rest of the Act for an indication. For example, where the section charged makes no reference to mens rea but other sections in the Act do, the offence could be considered strict liability: *Pharmaceutical Society of Great Britain v Storkwain* (1986). This is not an absolute rule however: see *Sherras v De Rutzen* (1895).

An offence is likely to be considered "truly criminal" where the penalty is a period of imprisonment. Lord Nichols in *B (a minor) v DPP* (2000) stated that if an offence carried more severe punishment and thus a graver stigma upon conviction, greater weight would be attached to the presumption in favour of mens rea. Regulatory offences are not considered to be truly criminal in the sense that they are to enforce standards rather than to enforce criminal law: *Wings Ltd v Ellis* (1984).

An issue of social concern can be considered to be where the offence covers any activity which is a "potential danger to public health, safety or morals" (Lord Diplock in *Sweet v Parsley*). Strict liability should only be imposed where it is promoting the effectiveness of the law. For example, in *Lim Chin Aik v The Queen* (1963) the Privy Council considered that strict liability would not assist in controlling illegal immigration when the defendant was charged with breaching an immigration order. Thus strict liability was not imposed in that case.

The approach outlined in *Gammon* has been followed in recent cases. In *B (a minor) v DPP* (2000), a 15-year-old boy was charged with having incited a girl under the age of 14 to commit an act of gross indecency with him, contrary to s.1(1) of the Indecency with Children Act 1960. The House of Lords followed the approach laid down in *Sweet v Parsley* and, applying the usual presumption in favour of a requirement for mens rea, held that for a conviction under the section, the prosecution had to prove that the defendant was not mistaken as to the victim's age. More precisely, the prosecution had to prove an absence of a genuine belief on the part of the accused, which did not have to be on reasonable grounds, that the victim was aged 14 or over. The presumption in favour of a requirement of mens rea is rebutted only if there is a compellingly clear implication that mens rea is not needed. Such an implication may be found in the language used in the wording of the offence, the nature of the offence, the mischief sought to be prevented and any other circumstances which may assist in determining what intention is properly to be attributed to Parliament when creating the offence.

The decision in *B v DPP* (2000) was followed and applied in *K* (2001) where D was charged with indecent assault on a girl under 16 and the House of Lords held that D's mistaken belief (whether reasonable or not) that the girl was over 16 was a valid defence. *B v DPP* and *K* have now been overtaken by the Sexual Offences Act 2003, which abolished a whole range of sexual offences, including those charged in these two cases, and enacted a new set of sexual offences. Now, in the case of a sexual offence against someone under 16, only a reasonable mistake that the victim is over 16 will be a defence: see Ch.8.

More recently, it was held in *R v M and Another* (2009), that the offence of bringing a prohibited article into prison contrary to s.40C(1)(a) of the Prison Act 1952 was not a strict liability offence. Utilising the principles from *Gammon* and *R v B*, the court reviewed the language in the Act and determined that, despite the fact that the statute contained some references to mens rea and there was no such reference to mens rea for the offence in question, this was not enough to rebut the presumption that mens rea was an essential ingredient of an offence.

SOME EXAMPLES OF STRICT LIABILITY OFFENCES

While there is no foolproof way of spotting in advance a strict liability crime, there are certain kinds of offence and certain types of wording used in statutes, which are more likely to lead to the imposition of strict liability.

Regulatory offences

One kind is the purely regulatory offence where no moral issue is at stake, the penalty is small, and from a practical point of view strict liability makes it easier to enforce these offences. Legislation relating to the sale of food provides a good example of this category: see *Smedleys Ltd v Breed* (1974), below.

Public danger offences

The second kind of offence is where the protection of the public is paramount. Here the penalty may be severe but strict liability is still deemed to be necessary to encourage the highest standard of care. The pollution cases are an example of this category, as are the dangerous drugs and weapons cases.

KEY CASE

STEELE (1993)
D was charged under s.1(1)(a) of the **Firearms Act 1968** with possession of a firearm without a certificate. He said that he had been given a holdall containing a sawn-off shotgun minutes before police arrived, and that he did not know what was in it. The Court of Appeal confirmed his conviction and said that it was irrelevant that he did not know, or even could not reasonably have known, what was in the bag. The legislation was obviously intended to be draconian.

Dangerous drugs

There are several crimes concerning dangerous drugs where liability is strict. These offences fall into the category of protection of public safety. In *Marriott* (1971), D was in possession of a penknife which he knew had traces of a substance on it. This substance turned out to be a prohibited drug. The court held that D needed mens rea with regard to possession of a substance on the knife, but no mens rea with regard to the circumstance that the substance was a prohibited drug. It did not matter that he did not know, and could not reasonably have known, what the substance was.

However, this general policy in the dangerous drugs cases has its limits: see *Sweet v Parsley*, above.

Road traffic offences

Some road traffic offences where strict liability is imposed are of a regulatory, quasi-criminal nature, while others are more serious. For example, the offence of driving with an amount of alcohol in the bloodstream which is over the proscribed limit is an offence contrary to s.5 of the **Road Traffic Act 1988**. Mens rea is not required with regard to the circumstance of having an amount of alcohol in the bloodstream over the proscribed limit. Similarly, the offences of driving whilst disqualified and driving without insurance do not require proof of mens rea. In *Bowsher* (1973), D was convicted of driving whilst disqualified even though he reasonably believed his disqualification had ended because his licence had been returned to him.

In *Williams* (2010), D was convicted of the more serious offence under s.3ZB of the **Road Traffic Act 1988** of causing death whilst driving without a licence and without insurance. D was driving his car on a dual carriageway when a pedestrian stepped out in front of him. There was nothing D could have done to avoid hitting the pedestrian, who died as a result of head injuries sustained in the collision. The Court of Appeal held that the offence did not require any fault on the part of the driver and D's appeal against conviction was dismissed. However, *Williams* was overruled by the Supreme Court in *Hughes* (2013). The Supreme Court ruled that, although the underlying offences of driving without insurance or without a licence are offences of strict liability, the aggravating element of causing death requires there to be some fault in the driving of the defendant (see Ch.1).

Pollution

Crimes involving pollution often provide other examples of strict liability crimes designed to protect the public. It is an offence under the Water Act 1989 to "cause" pollution of a river. Several cases have discussed the meaning of "cause" in this context. In *National Rivers Authority v Yorkshire Water Services* (1994) D operated a sewage works and one of its customers without D's knowledge discharged forbidden effluent through D's mechanisms. The Divisional Court held that "cause" does not imply either negligence or knowledge. Liability is, therefore, strict and D was liable.

Subsequently, in *Attorney General's Reference No. 1 of 1994* (1995), several Ds had been involved at various stages in operating a sewage system and toxic sewage had polluted the river contrary to s.107 of the **Water Act 1989**, due to a failure to properly maintain the system. The Court of Appeal held that such failure could amount to "causing" within the wording of the Act despite it being an omission rather than an act. Whereas the alternative charge of "permitting" was qualified by the word "knowingly", there was no such limit on "causing", for which liability was strict.

Sale of food

This is another regulatory area which, given the number of cases and the work of the inspectorate, it is felt is best kept under control by strict liability. The case of *Smedleys Ltd v Breed* (1974) provides an example. The D company was charged with selling food which was not of the substance demanded by the purchaser. A caterpillar had been found in a tin of peas from D's factory. The House of Lords held D liable even though there were no other practicable preventative measures which could have been taken and the standard of care taken at the factory was extremely high.

There are other areas where strict liability is prevalent, for example trade and industry, public health and liquor regulations.

DEFENCES

Some statutes imposing strict liability now contain a limited form of defence, often based on lack of negligence. It can be argued however, that this trend is turning crimes of strict liability into crimes of negligence. Whether one considers this desirable depends on how strongly one is convinced of the arguments for and against strict liability (see below).

For example, under s.21 of the Food Safety Act 1990, D has a defence if he shows that he took all reasonable precautions and exercised all due diligence to avoid the commission of the offence by himself or a person under his control. This defence is commonly found in relation to statutory offences designed to protect consumers for example, in the Trade Descriptions Act 1968 and the Consumer Protection Act 1987. It is in effect a "no negligence" defence with the burden of proof on the defendant to show that he was not negligent.

Reverse burdens of proof

Sometimes a reverse burden of proof is incompatible with the European Convention on Human Rights, in which case the statutory provision is interpreted to impose an evidential burden of proof on the defendant rather than a legal burden. This was the result in *Lambert* (2001) where it was held that Misuse of Drugs Act 1971 s.28(2) imposed an evidential burden on the accused. This section allowed the defendant a defence if he proved that he neither believed nor suspected nor had reason to suspect that the substance in his possession was a controlled drug. This was also the result where on a charge of professing to belong to a proscribed (terrorist) organisation, the statute provided that it was a defence for D to prove that he had not participated in the organisation's activities: *Att-Gen's Reference* (No.4 of 2002). On the other hand, where D was charged with driving when his blood alcohol level was above the prescribed limit, the House of Lords did not "read down" (i.e. interpret as an evidential burden) the legal burden on D to prove that there was no likelihood of his driving while in that condition: *Sheldrake* (2004).

REASONS IN FAVOUR OF STRICT LIABILITY

The main reasons in favour of imposing strict liability are:
(a) to protect the public from dangerous actions by creating a higher standard of care;
(b) to regulate quasi-criminal activities in as efficient a manner as possible;
(c) the law is easier to enforce as there is no requirement to prove mens rea and thus guilty pleas are more likely;
(d) lack of mens rea can be taken into account when sentencing.

In *Gammon (Hong Kong) Ltd v Attorney-General* (1984), the Privy Council felt that the reasons for displacing the requirement of mens rea in certain cases was to encourage a higher standard of vigilance and to ease administration. Strict liability can also facilitate the control of corporate crime. Crimes committed by corporations are often under-reported and under-prosecuted, despite the consequences, both in terms of money and life, although in recent years prosecutions have been more common. Strict liability can help the control of corporate crime because it dispenses in some respects with the often difficult task of imputing the necessary mens rea to a sufficiently senior official within a corporation: see Ch.4.

REASONS AGAINST STRICT LIABILITY

Those against strict liability offences argue that these offences impose penalties on persons who are not blameworthy in any way. In cases where there is not a "no negligence" defence, those who have taken care are still liable. There is no evidence to suggest that strict liability offences encourage higher standards and indeed some argue that it promotes lack of standards as you are bound to be found guilty whether you take care or not. Where the offence carries imprisonment, it could be argued that strict liability runs contrary to human rights principles.

PROPOSALS FOR REFORM

The Law Commission, in its report *The Mental Element in Crime* (1978), took the view that all crimes of strict liability should be treated as crimes of negligence. This would mean that any defendant charged with a strict liability offence would not be found guilty if he had taken all reasonable steps to prevent the action and thus had not been negligent. It would require Parliament to include no negligence defences more often when enacting strict liability offences.

In Australia, offences of strict liability have been mitigated by allowing a defence of all due care, the burden being on the defendant to prove his defence. This is one approach we have started to follow in this country and which could be more generally adopted, although it can raise human rights issues (see *Lambert*, above).

Another suggestion is to remove regulatory offences from the criminal courts and place them solely within the civil justice system. The Regulatory, Enforcement and Sanctions Act 2008 represents a move towards this as Pt III of the Act permits regulators to enforce sanctions, such as fines, for breaches of regulatory law. This would clearly not be suitable for drugs, firearms or sexual offences, which should obviously remain within the criminal justice system but moving regulatory offences in this way would alleviate some of the strain on the criminal courts.

This is not an area which attracts a lot of publicity or debate. Although many people think that there should be no strict liability and a minimum fault element of negligence should be required, others think the system works well in its present state and the administrative benefits outweigh any objections.

REVISION CHECKLIST

You should now know and understand:

☐ what a strict liability offence is;

☐ what an absolute liability offence is;

☐ the presumption in favour of mens rea;

☐ the criteria for displacing this presumption in order to find that an offence is one of strict liability;

☐ arguments for and against strict liability offences;

☐ proposals for reform.

Critically analyse the criteria utilised by the courts in determining whether an offence is one of strict liability.

This essay is asking you to consider the concept of strict liability and critically analyse the criteria used to determine if an offence is strict liability or not.

Suggested essay plan:

Introduction:
- Explain the concept of strict liability offences and difference between strict liability and absolute liability.
- Explain that there remains a presumption in favour of mens rea (*Sweet v Parsley*) but that this can be displaced in certain situations.
- The criteria to determine whether an offence is one of strict liability, where the Act is silent on the matter, is outlined in *Gammon*. State the criteria.
- Essay will analyse each of the criteria in turn.

Analyse: Presumption displaced if clearly or necessarily implied by effect of statute
- Presumption is displaced where there are clear words in the Act that no mens rea is required.
- Where the Act is silent, court looks to other sections in the Act. If there is reference to mens rea such as "recklessness" or "knowingly" in other sections, it is more likely that Parliament intended the silent section to be one of strict liability.
- Analyse whether this produces a consistent approach. Consider *Sherras v de Rutzen*.
- Consider whether this causes problems where there is no clear system in Act – *K*.

Analyse: Presumption strong where offence is "truly criminal"

- Explain the rules that a serious offence is more likely to require mens rea. Notion of only punishing those who are committing crimes with forethought.
- Where an offence carries imprisonment, this is less likely to be an offence of strict liability. This is not a strict rule.
- Analyse whether this rule is fair.

Analyse: Impose strict liability where offence involves issue of "social concern"

- Explain that this applies where the offence covers activity which is a potential danger to public health.
- No precise definition of "social concern" and this is not a clear rule. *Sweet v Parsley* refers to crimes such as those where there is a potential danger to public health, safety or morals.
- Analyse the situation relating to wireless transmissions (*Blake*). Consider whether these are truly an issue of social concern.

Analyse: Strict liability should be effective in promoting the law

- Explain that the courts should not impose strict liability where it does not assist in upholding the law (*Lim Chin Aik*).
- Analyse whether this encourages greater vigilance to prevent offending.
- Query whether strict liability can be capable of promoting the law— if D is going to be convicted regardless of any preventative measures taken, arguably there is no need to take those measures.

Conclude: Form overall conclusion.

Multiple parties to a crime

. . . .

INTRODUCTION

This chapter is concerned with the situation where there is more than one person involved in the commission of a criminal offence. In such a case, both the perpetrator and the other participants in the offence may all be jointly liable for the crime. This chapter will explain how the law apportions liability for multiple participants.

. . . .

PRINCIPAL OFFENDER

The principal is the main perpetrator of the offence. He is the one who commits the actus reus or a substantial part of the actus reus. It is possible to have more than one principal if more than one person is directly responsible for the actus reus. An example of this is where two people together break into a warehouse and steal items from inside. The defendants in this situation are considered *joint principals* and the offence is considered to be a *joint enterprise*. It does not matter who actually carried out the actus reus of the offence, as long as all parties were present and helped to carry out the plan. In this case, all parties may be jointly charged as principals.

Where it appears that a second person is not directly responsible for the actus reus but had a part to play in the commission of the offence, they will be liable as a secondary party. The test to establish whether someone is a joint principal or merely a secondary party is whether they participate in the actus reus by their own independent act rather than by adopting a supporting role. Where a supporting role is clearly adopted, the secondary party is more likely to be charged as an accessory to the crime but even if liable in this way, he will nevertheless be treated as a principal (see below on secondary parties).

Innocent agents

A principal may not always directly carry out the actus reus himself. He may use another person, who is unaware of the crime being committed, to do the act. This person is deemed an *innocent agent* as they can be considered to lack mens rea for the offence. A good example of this is the case of *R v*

Cogan; *R v Leak* (1976) where L forced his wife to have sex with another man, C. C's rape conviction was quashed on the basis that he honestly believed L's wife was consenting, while L's conviction was upheld. L caused the rape to happen even though he was not a direct participant in the actus reus.

Another way in which the actus reus can be committed by an innocent agent is where that person has a defence. For example, if Audrey asked Ben to break into a locked house belonging to Jim, telling Ben that the house was hers but she had locked herself out, Ben can be considered an innocent agent in the burglary. He can rely on the defence of mistake to negate mens rea and Audrey is considered the principal in the burglary.

SECONDARY PARTIES

A person is considered a secondary party to an offence if they help or encourage the principal either *before* the offence is committed by the principal or *at the time* the offence is committed. As outlined above, they do not normally take part directly in the commission of the actus reus and will be charged as an accessory.

Liability for secondary parties in indictable offences is established under s.8 of the Accessories and Abettors Act 1861 as amended by the Criminal Law Act 1977:

LEGISLATION HIGHLIGHTER

Accessories and Abettors Act 1861 s.8

"Whosoever shall aid, abet, counsel or procure the commission of any indictable offence, whether the same be an offence at common law or by virtue of any Act passed or to be passed, shall be liable to be tried, indicted and punished as a principal offender."

Section 44 of the Magistrates' Courts Act 1980 makes a similar provision with respect to summary offences. Secondary parties will therefore be treated in the same way as the principal offender, although where there is discretion in sentencing, their degree of involvement may be taken into account.

Assistance after the offence

Assistance given after the commission of the offence, for example, to enable someone to escape or dispose of evidence, does not come within the scope of secondary liability. It is a separate offence intentionally to impede the apprehension or prosecution of an arrestable offender (s.4 of the Criminal Law Act 1967 (CLA 1967)).

ESTABLISHING THE LIABILITY OF A SECONDARY PARTY

Firstly, the principal must actually have committed the offence (sometimes just the actus reus of it) before anyone can be liable as a secondary party. If the actus reus has not been committed, consider inchoate liability: see Ch.5.

Actus reus of the secondary party

For a secondary party to be liable, it must be proved that he participated by either aiding, abetting, counselling or procuring the principal in the commission of the offence. These four words have been held to have distinct meanings although there is considerable overlap between them. Thus it is possible for one person to participate in an offence in a number of different ways.

KEY CASE

ATTORNEY GENERAL'S REFERENCE NO. 1 OF 1975
The principal offender was driving with a blood-alcohol level over the prescribed limit. The secondary party had added alcohol to the principal's drink without his knowledge, knowing that he would be driving. Lord Widgery C.J. confirmed that the words in s.8 of the 1861 Act should be given their ordinary meaning where possible and that there is clearly a difference between them otherwise Parliament would not have used all four words. Some general comments were made about secondary participation and the distinctions between the four modes of secondary participation.

Aiding

This is helping or assisting the principal to commit the offence and it requires more than mere knowledge. Aiding must occur either before or during the commission of the offence. Examples are keeping watch or providing the gun used in a shooting.

Abetting

This is providing encouragement to the principal at the time of the offence. In *Giannetto* (1997) the Court of Appeal stated that this involved anything "from mere encouragement upwards". Thus, it would appear crucial that the abettor is present at the scene of the crime. A person may be guilty of abetting by presence alone if his presence provided encouragement in fact and he intended to provide encouragement through his presence.

MULTIPLE PARTIES TO A CRIME

KEY CASE

WILCOX V JEFFREY (1951)

An American saxophonist played a concert in London. His entry into the United Kingdom was conditional upon him not taking up employment while he remained in the country. D owned the magazine *Jazz Illustrated* and had met the saxophonist at the airport, attended the concert and subsequently provided a very positive review in the magazine. D was convicted of abetting the illegal concert due to his voluntary presence in the crowd and this was upheld on appeal.

A person can also be considered an abettor by omitting to act. This will be the case where D has knowledge of the actions of the principal and also has a duty or right to control those actions but deliberately fails to do anything about it. In *Tuck v Robson* (1970) D was a pub landlord who failed to remove three late drinkers from his pub. He was convicted of aiding and abetting the customers to consume alcohol outside licensed hours under the Licensing Act 1964 by being present in the pub, knowing what the three customers were doing and failing to take steps to prevent it.

Counselling

This involves giving advice prior to the commission of the crime. Thus the counsellor may well not be present at the scene of the crime.

KEY CASE

CALHAEM (1985)

D was charged with murder. She was said to have counselled Z to commit murder. Z gave evidence that despite D's instructions he had no intention of carrying out the killing. However, when he got to the victim's flat he had gone "berserk" and killed her. The jury was directed that counselling involved "putting somebody up to something" and that the acts carried out must be within the scope of the instructions. D was convicted and appealed on the basis that the jury should have been directed that there had to be a causal connection between the counselling and the act, and here there was not. The court rejected this argument and upheld the conviction. It was confirmed that for counselling, there must be (1) contact between the parties, (2) a connection between the counselling and offence committed, and (3) the act done must be within the scope of the authority or advice.

Procuring

This means to "produce by endeavour", i.e. to ensure that something happens and take steps to produce the outcome: see *Cogan & Leak* (1976), above. It is unnecessary for the principal to know about the procuring, but procuring does require a causal connection between the principal's commission of the offence and the action of D. In *Attorney General's Reference No. 1 of 1975* (above), the procuring was without the knowledge and consent of the principal but was nonetheless the cause of the offence.

Mens rea of the secondary party

The secondary party must (1) intend to aid, abet, counsel or procure the principal to commit the offence and, (2) have knowledge of the circumstances which constitute the offence.

Intention

D must intend to participate in the commission of the offence and intention is given its usual meaning, i.e. aim, purpose or desire. Equally, foresight of the consequences as being a virtually certain outcome of D's actions can be evidence of intent (oblique intent). It is no defence that D was completely indifferent as to whether or not the offence would be committed: *Bryce* (2004).

Knowledge of circumstances of offence

Secondary participants need both mens rea as to their own actus reus (aiding, abetting, counselling or procuring) and knowledge of, or at least wilful blindness as to, the circumstances of the substantive offence. This is so even in relation to strict liability offences. In *Johnson v Youden and Others* (1950) Lord Goddard C.J. stated that a person could only be convicted as an accessory if he knew, at least, the essential matters which constitute the offence committed. This is the *contemplation principle* and it was developed in the case of *Bainbridge* (1960).

KEY CASE

BAINBRIDGE (1960)

D had purchased some oxygen-cutting equipment on behalf of a third party who he knew was going to use it for an illegal purpose, although he was not sure what that purpose was. The court held that D, to be liable, would need to know more than that the purpose was illegal. Although he did not need to know all of the precise details, he would need to know that a crime of that kind was going to be committed, for example here, that the equipment was going to be used for breaking and entering.

Thus the secondary party need not know all the details of the offence to be committed but he must know the type of offence or have a range of possible offences in mind.

KEY CASE

DPP for Northern Ireland v Maxwell (1978)

D was a member of a terrorist organisation. He was told to drive some men to a cinema. He knew that their purpose was illegal but he did not know the specific details. In fact they planted a bomb. He was convicted of abetting an act done with intent to cause an unlawful explosion. The House of Lords held that he did not need to know the precise weapon and method to be used by the others. He knew they were terrorists. He knew their purpose would be to endanger life or property. That was enough. Lord Scarman stated, "A man will not be convicted of aiding and abetting any offence his principal may commit but only one which is within his contemplation. He may have in contemplation only one offence, or several; and the several which he contemplates he may see as alternatives. An accessory that leaves it to his principal to choose is liable, provided always the choice is made from the range of offences from which the accessory contemplates the choice will be made." Lord Fraser referred to, "the range of crimes any of which he must have known were to be expected that night".

SUMMARY OF SECONDARY LIABILITY

ACTUS REUS
D must do one of the following:
- **Aid:** assist at time of or before offence (*Bainbridge*)
- **Abet:** encourage at time of offence (*Wilcox v Jeffrey*)
- **Counsel:** advise before offence (*Calhaem*)
- **Procure:** produce by endeavour (*Cogan & Leak*)

MENS REA
D must possess both of the following:
- **Intention** to aid, abet, counsel or procure
- **Knowledge/contemplation** of the offence or range of possible offences (*Bainbridge, Maxwell*)

JOINT ENTERPRISE

As stated above, a joint enterprise is where two or more people embark upon a criminal enterprise to commit a particular offence together, as a team. While a distinction was drawn by the Court of Appeal in *Stewart and Schofield* (1995) between joint enterprise and secondary liability, the leading authority is now *Powell and English* (1997) in which no support was given for this notion. Therefore the approach now taken is that joint enterprise is simply part of the law of secondary liability. For this reason, a secondary party may be charged as an accessory where he aids, abets, counsels or procures the principal rather than directly taking part in the actus reus himself. Equally, he may be charged as a principal under the joint enterprise rules where he takes a more active part in carrying out the actus reus. The latter may also be the case where there are two people present at the scene of the crime but it is not clear who committed the act and who helped. An example is *Mohan v R.* (1967) where it was not clear which of the two Ds struck the fatal blow to the victim. Both were convicted of murder as a joint enterprise (joint principals).

In a joint enterprise, all parties are jointly liable for crimes committed by any of them. This creates a problem where two persons have set out on a joint enterprise and one of them does something unplanned. For example, John and Bill break into a house at night with intent to steal expensive paintings in the property (burglary) but they are confronted by the householder. If Bill takes out a knife and stabs the householder violently, to what extent can John be held liable as principal for the GBH offence committed by Bill?

In *Anderson*; *Morris* (1966) Lord Parker C.J. clarified the position, stating that all parties are liable for the acts of each other provided they arise from the execution of the agreed joint enterprise. However if one person goes beyond what is agreed, the co-accused is not liable for the unauthorised act where it is a complete departure from the plan. More recent cases have focussed on the *contemplation principle*, which implies that where one party foresees that the other might commit a different offence in the course of the joint enterprise, they are jointly liable for that other offence.

Therefore, in this situation, a number of requirements must be satisfied before D can be liable as a joint principal.

1. D must have foreseen that the principal would commit the actus reus of the other offence and that the principal would do so with the requisite mens rea for that offence.

2. The principal's act must be within the "scope of the joint enterprise".

KEY CASE

RAHMAN & OTHERS (2008)

Four appellants had attacked a 16-year-old boy using a variety of blunt objects, including baseball bats and metal bars. The fatal wounds were caused by two blows with a knife in the back. It could not be proven who had inflicted the knife wounds but it was probably someone who had escaped and was not apprehended. All four appellants denied knowledge of the knife but all were convicted of murder. Their appeals to both Court of Appeal and House of Lords were dismissed. Their Lordships stated that to face liability for murder in a joint enterprise case where V had been killed by one party, D did not have to foresee that E *would* kill with intent to kill. The court must look at what the defendant foresaw their associate *might* do in such a case.

In joint enterprise cases involving weapons, it is important to consider whether D knew that the other party was armed and, if so, with what weapon. If D did have this knowledge in advance, it is easier to prove that he foresaw the possibility that the other might kill.

KEY CASE

POWELL, ENGLISH (1997)

In *Powell*, P and D and one other man visited a drug dealer. One of them, possibly the third man, killed the drug dealer. In *English*, W and E took part in a joint enterprise to attack a police officer (V) with wooden posts. During the attack, W produced a knife and stabbed V to death. There was a reasonable possibility that E did not know that W was armed with a knife. P and E were convicted of murder as secondary parties.

The House of Lords held (1) it is sufficient to found a conviction for murder, for a secondary party to have realised that in the course of the joint enterprise, the principal might kill with intent to do so or with intent to cause grievous bodily harm; (2) where, however, the principal offender kills with a deadly weapon which the secondary party did not know that he had and therefore did not foresee the use of, the secondary party is not guilty of murder. However:

> "... if the weapon used by the primary party is different to, but as dangerous as, the weapon which the secondary party contemplated he might use, the secondary party should not escape liability for murder because of the difference in the weapon, for example, if he foresaw that the primary party might use a gun to kill and the latter used a knife to kill, or *vice versa*."

Therefore, the position is that the principal's act must be an act contemplated by D, i.e. not fundamentally different from any kind of act foreseen by D. D has no criminal liability at all in respect of the principal's acts which are outside the scope of the joint enterprise, e.g. where D foresees only the use of fists to beat up the intended victim and the principal attacks the victim using a lethal weapon which D did not even contemplate the principal had.

Even though the principal offender can be liable for murder only if he intended death or grievous bodily harm, the secondary offender does not have to have had such an intention. Nor does he have to have "authorised" or "agreed to" the principal's actions. It is sufficient that he took part in the enterprise, with foresight that the principal might kill with the requisite mens rea, i.e. intention. The same is true in the case of an attempted crime, where the principal offender can be guilty only if he intended to commit the full offence but another person can be convicted provided he participated in the enterprise with foresight that the principal offender might intentionally attempt the full offence: *O'Brien* (1995).

The difficult application of transferred malice (see Ch.2) to joint liability was considered by the Supreme Court in *Gnango* (2011).

KEY CASE

GNANGO, 2011

D voluntarily took part in an exchange of gunfire with B in a public place. A shot fired by B killed an innocent passer-by (V). B was never caught and D was charged with V's murder. At D's trial, the judge directed the jury that D would be liable for murder if the jury was sure that D and B had been engaged in a joint enterprise to shoot at one another and D realised that, in the course of the joint enterprise, B might kill another with the requisite mens rea for murder. D was convicted of murder.

The Court of Appeal quashed D's conviction on the basis that the shooting of V had gone beyond the common purpose of D and B, i.e. to shoot at each other and to be shot at. The Prosecution appealed to the Supreme Court, arguing that D had aided and abetted the commission of the murder by actively encouraging B to shoot at him.

The Supreme Court reinstated D's conviction. D and B had voluntarily engaged in a gunfight with each other, each intending to kill or cause GBH to the other, and each foreseeing that the other had the reciprocal intention. D was liable for murder when B mistakenly shot V in the course of the gunfight. The Court reasoned that D had aided, abetted, counselled and/or procured B to shoot at him and was, therefore, guilty of aiding and abetting his own attempted murder.

> Under the doctrine of transferred malice, B was liable for murder when he accidentally shot V instead of D. Under the same doctrine, by aiding and abetting B to shoot at him, D was a party to the murder of V.

Where the secondary party, e.g. in a joint enterprise situation, is not a party to the act of the principal offender (e.g. where the principal offender uses a weapon which the secondary party did not even foresee he had), then the secondary party is not liable at all in respect of the act of the principal offender. Apart from that situation, it is possible for the secondary party to be guilty of the same offence as the principal offender or of a greater or lesser offence, depending on the mens rea of the secondary party: *Gilmour* (2000). Thus in homicide, where the secondary party is party to the principal's act, but does not foresee that the principal offender might kill with intent to do so or with intent to cause grievous bodily harm, then the secondary party could be guilty of the lesser offence of manslaughter, provided the secondary party foresaw that the principal offender might inflict actual bodily harm.

KEY CASE

STEWART AND SCHOFIELD (1995)
Ds went with a third party to carry out a robbery, taking a pole. The third party beat the victim to death with the pole and was convicted of murder. The Ds were convicted of manslaughter. They appealed claiming that they should have been convicted of murder or nothing. Dismissing their appeal, the Court of Appeal held that in a joint enterprise case where the secondary party was party to the fatal act but only had mens rea appropriate for a lesser offence, he would be liable for that lesser offence.

ACQUITTAL OF PRINCIPAL OFFENDER

If there is no principal offender convicted of the offence, this does not necessarily present a problem in convicting a secondary party. Providing it can be proved that an offence or, at least, the actus reus of an offence was committed, a secondary participant can still be convicted.

Acquittal due to lack of actus reus
If a principal offender is acquitted because the court is satisfied that no actus reus of an offence has been committed, then there can be no secondary liability. In *Thornton v Mitchell* (1940), a bus conductor was charged as a

secondary party to careless driving after helping a driver to reverse. The driver was acquitted on the basis of a lack of carelessness. The conductor was acquitted too. If there was no careless driving, there could be no aiding and abetting of it.

Acquittal due to lack of mens rea or due to valid defence

If there is an actus reus committed there can still be secondary liability even if the alleged principal offender is not guilty due to lack of mens rea or because he has a valid defence.

KEY CASE

COGAN AND LEAK (1976)

D had persuaded a friend to have intercourse with his (D's) wife. The friend had honestly but unreasonably believed the wife was consenting and was therefore (on the law as it then was) not guilty of rape. However, the actus reus of rape had been committed. Thus it was possible for a secondary party who had not believed in the wife's consent to be liable. Such was D but he was also her husband and a husband at that time could not be guilty of raping his wife. The court nevertheless upheld his conviction on two alternative bases: (i) he was liable as secondary party for procuring the commission of the actus reus by his friend; (ii) he was liable as a principal offender acting through the innocent agency of his friend. [Note that a husband can now be guilty as principal offender of rape of his wife: *R* (1992).]

KEY CASE

MILLWARD (1994)

D, knowing that his vehicle was defective, instructed B, his employee to drive it. A fatal accident occurred because of the defect. B was acquitted of causing death by reckless driving but D was convicted. On appeal, D's conviction was upheld on the basis that he had procured the commission of the actus reus of the offence. A procurer can be guilty even though the principal is not guilty because of lack of mens rea.

KEY CASE

BOURNE (1952)

D forced his wife on two separate occasions to commit buggery with a dog. He was convicted of aiding and abetting the offence even though his wife, the principal, could not be convicted (had she been prosecuted) due to his duress. The actus reus and mens rea of buggery had been carried out.

Thus, the key is the performance of the actus reus of the offence by the principal.

WITHDRAWAL FROM PARTICIPATION

If an alleged secondary party repents before the offence is committed then he may escape liability if he withdraws at a sufficiently early stage, communicates that withdrawal unequivocally to the other participant(s) and does all that he reasonably can to avert commission of the crime. The extent of the latter requirement depends upon how advanced the commission of the crime is. As stated by McDermott J. in *Eldridge v United States* 623 F2d449 (1932), "A declared intent to withdraw from a conspiracy to dynamite a building is not enough, if the fuse has been set; he must step on the fuse". Whether there has been a withdrawal is a question for the court to decide on the facts of the case before them.

KEY CASE

BECERRA & COOPER (1975)

D and E were engaged on a joint enterprise to commit burglary of a flat. The householder confronted them, which caused the neighbour upstairs to investigate what was going on. When confronted by the neighbour, D shouted, "Come on, let's go!", climbed out of the flat window and ran away. E was prevented from leaving by the neighbour and E stabbed him to death. Both D and E were convicted of murder. D appealed on the ground that he had withdrawn from the joint enterprise by the time that E stabbed the victim. The Court of Appeal stated that something "vastly different and vastly more effective" was required from D before he could escape liability.

The communication of withdrawal must be "unequivocal". This was confirmed in the case of *Baker* (1994). In this case, D had initially taken part in a knife attack, then stopped, turned away and said that he no longer wanted to carry out the attack. The court held that this was not enough to avoid liability. D had to dissociate himself completely from the crime occurring at all, and not just from his part in it. What constitutes effective withdrawal depends on the facts of each case and is for the jury to decide.

An unequivocal communication to the other parties is not necessary in the case of spontaneous (as opposed to pre-planned) violence. In such a situation, simply walking away will be sufficient, although it will not absolve D from criminal liability for any acts committed while he was still a party to the violence: *Mitchell* (1998).

Where death has resulted and D is charged with being a party to murder, D is not guilty unless it is established that the fatal injuries were inflicted while D was still acting within the joint enterprise. In *O'Flaherty, Ryan and Toussant* (2004), a street fight occurred between two groups of men. One group included O, R, T and others. O, R and T used weapons (a cricket bat, a hammer and a beer bottle). When the fight moved to a nearby street, R and T did not follow. The deceased, H, who was a member of the other group, died from injuries received. In the second street, O, still holding the cricket bat, was seen to move within a few feet of H's prone body, although he was not seen to use the bat at this stage. There was no evidence that any injury causative of death was inflicted in the first street. R and T's convictions were quashed because a person who disengages from the joint enterprise before the commission of the crime is not liable for that crime. O's conviction was upheld. He was present and at least providing encouragement.

PROPOSALS FOR REFORM

In its Report No. 305 *Participating in Crime* (2007), The Law Commission recommended replacing the common law rules on secondary liability and innocent agency with a statutory scheme of offences. The new offences would catch someone who "assists" or "encourages", thus, the intention would be that "counselling" and "procuring" would no longer be part of the terminology of secondary offences.

It was proposed that a new secondary liability offence be introduced which would be committed where D assisted or encouraged the commission of an offence. Encouraging would be where D emboldens, threatens or pressurises someone to commit an offence. This offence could be committed by omission and D must intend that the conduct element of the substantive offence (actus reus) be committed. This proposal has been partially accepted: see Ch.5.

The report recommended the retention of the principle of innocent agency. Thus, D would be liable as a principal offender if he intentionally caused an innocent agent, P, to commit the conduct element of the principal offence. P would be an innocent agent if the only reason that he was not himself guilty of the offence was that he was under 10, had a defence of insanity or acted without the fault element (the mens rea) for the offence.

The report recommended retaining the principle of joint enterprise. However, it is suggested that the mens rea for joint enterprise should be changed so that D is liable for a "joint criminal venture" where he intends or believes that E should, would or might commit the conduct element (actus reus) of the substantive offence. He would not be liable, however, despite having this intent, if the conduct fell outside of the scope of the joint venture.

By way of defences, the proposals would (a) retain the defence (as in *Tyrrell* (1894)) for a victim who is in a class of persons whom an offence was intended to protect, and (b) provide a defence for someone acting reasonably to prevent the commission of an offence or the occurrence of harm (e.g. diverting P's intention to injure someone into an intention instead to damage property).

Apart from the proposal relating to assisting and encouraging crime, the remaining proposals have not been implemented.

REVISION CHECKLIST

You should now know and understand:

- [ ] who is considered to be the principal in the commission of an offence;
- [ ] the concept of joint liability and when it will apply;
- [ ] who is considered to be a secondary party in the commission of an offence;
- [ ] how secondary parties are dealt with by the courts;
- [ ] what is required to establish secondary liability;
- [ ] when the secondary liability principles will apply;
- [ ] what is a joint enterprise
- [ ] what is required for withdrawal from a joint enterprise.

QUESTION

Angus shows Charles how to pick a lock. He does not know exactly what Charles intends to do, although he knows he is going to "sort out" his boss, who owes him money.

Charles breaks into his boss' house and takes a painting which he estimates is of the same value as the money he is owed. He is charged with burglary and Angus is charged as a secondary party. Charles' defence is that he thought he had a right to do what he did, as he saw it as the only way of getting what he was owed. Angus' defence is that he did not know exactly what Charles would do but he thought he would simply try to get his money back.

Advise Angus and Charles as to their criminal liability, if any, and the availability of any defences.

ADVICE AND THE ANSWER

You should first identify the relevant offence arising from the facts of the scenario and then identify who may be responsible for the commission of that offence. Here we are dealing with a potential burglary and the two possible offenders are Charles and Angus. As it appears that Charles has committed the most significant part of the offence, consider his liability as principal first and thereafter consider if, and how, Angus might be liable.

Answer guide

Charles

Has he committed burglary (considered in Ch.10)? **Theft Act 1968** s.9(1)(a) requires entry as a trespasser with intent to commit theft/ GBH/criminal damage. Explore actus reus elements— it appears that Charles has entered a building/part of a building (his boss' house) as a trespasser (he did not have permission and knew that he did not have permission). Consider mens rea elements—what was his intent when he entered? If on entering he did not intend to commit the theft, then he is not guilty under s.9(1)(a). If he committed theft subsequently, he can be liable for burglary under s.9(1)(b) which requires proof of entry to a building/part of a building as a trespasser (considered above) plus the commission of theft or an attempted theft.

So, for s.9(1)(b) burglary, now consider the actus reus elements of theft— it appears that Charles has appropriated (taking the painting is assuming the rights of owner) property (painting) belonging to another (his boss). Consider mens rea elements of theft—has Charles done so dishonestly and with intent to permanently deprive? In relation to the former, Charles may claim that he is not dishonest because he believed he had a right in law under s.2. If so, this would mean that he is not guilty of theft and thus not guilty of burglary by virtue of **Theft Act 1968** s.2. However, was this belief that he had a right in law or just a moral right? Belief in a moral right does not preclude dishonesty. Consider the *Ghosh* test to establish dishonesty. It appears he had an intention to permanently deprive as he intended the painting to replace the money owed to him.

Angus

Consider liability as a secondary party. Was Angus aiding, abetting, counselling or procuring Charles in his commission of the burglary (*Att-Gen's Ref No.1 of 1975*)? Angus may have committed the actus reus of aiding (assisting by teaching Charles how to pick a lock). He may have been counselling Charles (providing encouragement in the demonstration of how to pick a lock). Consider the mens rea required of a secondary party. Angus must intend to aid, abet, counsel or procure and it appears that he does have that intention in relation to his demonstration. However, does Angus have sufficient knowledge of the offence committed by Charles? He needs to know the kind of offence being committed but not necessarily the full details (*Bainbridge, Maxwell*). Does Angus have to foresee the actus reus of the full offence, or does he have to foresee that Charles may commit the actus reus with the necessary mens rea *(Powell, English)*? It may not be enough in these circumstances to prove secondary liability as Angus did not know that Charles would do something illegal although it is questionable that Angus could assume that some sort of breaking and entering was going to take place. Even if Charles is not liable for burglary due to lack of mens rea, Angus can still be liable as a secondary party if the requirements are proven.

Inchoate offences

. . . .

INTRODUCTION

Inchoate literally translated means "at an early stage". Inchoate offences are crimes where D has not actually committed a substantive offence but has taken steps towards committing it. Such an offence will be committed where D does one of the following:

- *Attempts* to commit an offence
- Enters into a *conspiracy* with at least one other person to commit an offence
- *Assists or encourages* someone else to commit a crime (but unlike secondary liability, the crime has not been committed)

Inchoate offences therefore cover the preparatory stages of other criminal offences. They are substantive offences in themselves and, unlike liability for secondary participation in a crime, it is not necessary that the main offence be committed. Indeed it is often unlikely, and in some cases impossible, that it will be committed.

. . . .

ATTEMPTS

The law relating to liability for attempts is now governed by the Criminal Attempts Act 1981.

LEGISLATION HIGHLIGHTER

Criminal Attempts Act 1981 s.1(1)

"If, with intent to commit an offence to which this section applies, a person does an act which is more than merely preparatory to the commission of the offence, he is guilty of attempting to commit the offence."

Section 1 applies to both indictable and either way offences thus it is a crime to attempt to commit such offences. It is not a crime to attempt to commit a summary offence.

Actus reus of attempt

The actus reus of an attempt is doing an act which is "more than merely preparatory" to the commission of an offence. The question of whether an act is more than merely preparatory is a question of fact to be left to the jury (**Criminal Attempts Act 1981** s.4(3)). The judge must not usurp the jury's function. Thus, where there is evidence of an attempt, the issue must be left to the jury. The question of what constitutes an attempt (an act more than merely preparatory) has been an issue that the courts have debated over the years.

"Proximity" test: This test was used prior to the 1981 Act to define an attempt. The test looked back from the complete offence and asked whether D's acts were so immediately connected with the actus reus that liability should be imposed for an attempt (*Eagleton* (1855)).

"Rubicon" test: In *Widdowson* (1986) the Court used a test set out in *DPP v Stonehouse* (1978) which indicated that proximity could be gauged by whether D's acts constituted "a fixed irrevocable intention to go on to commit the complete offence unless involuntarily prevented from doing so. [D] must have crossed the Rubicon and burnt his boats."

"Series of acts" test: This test states that an attempt to commit a crime is "an act done with intent to commit that crime, and forming part of a series of acts which would constitute its actual commission if it were not interrupted": *Boyle & Boyle* (1987).

These tests were combined in the case of *Gullefer* (1986) in an effort to create a decisive view on the issue.

KEY CASE

GULLEFER (1986)

D placed a bet on a greyhound race and subsequently tried to distract the dogs in order to get a call of "no race" and so retrieve his stake. He was charged with attempted theft. The case turned on whether what he had done was "more than merely preparatory" to the commission of the theft. At trial the "Rubicon test" (has D "burnt his boats" and reached the point of no return?) was referred to. On appeal this test was rejected on the basis that the specific pre-1981 tests no longer applied. In the view of Lord Lane, "The words of the [1981] Act seek to steer a midway course" between the *Eagleton* test (proximity) and the point of no return (*Rubicon*). The Act is a guide as to when the "series of acts" (*Boyle & Boyle*) starts and that is when D *"embarks on a crime proper"*.

This approach was followed in *Jones* (1990) and expanded upon in *Geddes* (1996).

GEDDES (1996)

D had entered the grounds of a school and was found in the boys' toilet by a member of staff. He ran away discarding a rucksack containing lengths of string, sealing tape, a knife and other items. He was convicted of attempting to falsely imprison a person unknown and appealed. The Court of Appeal held that, although he undoubtedly had the necessary intention, the evidence showed no more than that he had made preparations, got himself ready and put himself in a position to commit the offence of false imprisonment. He had not moved from the role of preparation into that of execution or implementation.

Lord Bingham C.J. stated, "There is no rule of thumb test. There must always be an exercise of judgment based on the particular facts of the case". The test adopted was one where it is asked whether the evidence demonstrates that D has done an act which shows he actually tried to commit the offence or whether he only put himself in a position to do so.

Therefore, activities such as getting equipped for a burglary by purchasing bolt cutters, undertaking reconnaissance of the scene, lying in wait for the security guards to go off duty, etc. will not amount to anything more than preparation. However, moving towards the gate of the factory yard and starting to cut the lock on the gate is likely to be considered evidence of an attempted burglary. An example is the case of *Tosti and White* (1997). The Ds obtained oxyacetylene equipment, drove to the scene of a planned burglary, concealed the equipment in a hedge, approached the door of a barn and examined the padlock on it. At that point they realised they were being watched and ran off. They appealed against their convictions for attempted burglary. It was held, dismissing their appeal, that there was evidence that they had done an act which showed that they had actually attempted to commit the offence. The judge had been correct to leave the issue to the jury and the jury were entitled to find them guilty.

Mens rea for attempts

The mens rea of an attempt is D's intention to commit an offence: Criminal Attempts Act 1981 s.1(1). Attempt is therefore a crime of specific intent and recklessness will not suffice. So D will be guilty of attempted theft, for example, where he does an act more than merely preparatory towards committing the actus reus of theft and does so with intent to commit theft. On a charge of attempted murder, although intention to commit GBH will suffice as the mens rea for murder, it must be proved that D did an act more than merely preparatory towards committing murder, with intent to kill: *Whybrow* (1951). An intention to commit GBH would constitute attempted GBH only.

KEY CASE

MOHAN (1976)

D refused to stop his car when a police officer signalled him to do so. Instead he drove straight at the officer, who managed to avoid him. He was convicted of attempting to cause grievous bodily harm. His conviction was quashed because the jury had been misdirected regarding the mens rea for attempt. The Court of Appeal defined the necessary mens rea as intention, in other words:

> "a decision to bring about, insofar as it lies within the accused's power, the commission of the offence which it is alleged the accused attempted to commit, no matter whether the accused desired that consequence or not."

This excludes recklessness and foresight of probable or likely consequences. However, the mens rea can take the form of oblique intent as outlined in *Nedrick, Woollin*, etc. In *Walker and Hayles* (1990) the Ds had thrown their victim from a third-floor balcony and seriously injured him. They were convicted of attempted murder and appealed on the basis that the meaning of intention in attempts was restricted to purpose or direct intent. The Court of Appeal, upholding their convictions, made it clear that intention can include oblique intent.

The mens rea requirement of intent, rather than recklessness, does not apply to the circumstances of an offence. Thus it is possible to attempt to commit an offence even though D was reckless as to some elements of the actus reus.

KEY CASE

ATTORNEY GENERAL'S REFERENCE NO.3 OF 1992 (1994)

The Ds were charged with attempted aggravated arson, i.e. attempting to damage property and being reckless as to whether the life of another would be endangered thereby. They threw a petrol bomb from a moving car at a stationary car and the bomb hit a pavement and a wall. There was no evidence that they intended to endanger life. The Court of Appeal held that recklessness as to the circumstances of endangering life was sufficient for liability for attempted aggravated arson, provided they intended to cause the criminal damage.

Attempting the impossible

Criminal Attempts Act 1981 s.1(2) and (3)

s.1(2) "A person may be guilty of attempting to commit an offence to which this section applies even though the facts are such that the commission of the offence is impossible."

s.1(3) "In any case where—
   (a) apart from this subsection a person's intention would not be regarded as having amounted to an intention to commit an offence; but
   (b) if the facts of the case had been as he believed them to be, his intention would be so regarded,
   then for the purposes of subsection (1)... he shall be regarded as having had an intention to commit an offence."

A person can attempt the impossible and this is the case irrespective of whether the crime is physically impossible (e.g. attempting to steal from an empty handbag) or legally impossible (e.g. attempting to supply talcum powder believing it to be a class A controlled drug). Despite the position clearly set out in the 1981 Act, the first case to go to the House of Lords on this point resulted in a surprising interpretation of the Act.

KEY CASE

ANDERTON V RYAN (1985)
D was charged with attempting to dishonestly handle a video recorder. D had received it believing it to be stolen but the police could not produce positive evidence that it was stolen and the case had to proceed on the basis that it was not. The House of Lords held that no section of the Act made it an offence to attempt to do something which, if the defendant had done all he intended to do, would not have been a crime. That was the case here.

The case of *Shivpuri* (1986) has now overruled *Anderton v Ryan* and reinterpreted the Act. Lord Bridge, who gave one of the leading judgments in *Anderton v Ryan* also gave judgment in *Shivpuri* and the issues were reassessed.

KEY CASE

SHIVPURI (1986)

D was convicted of attempting to be knowingly concerned in dealing with a prohibited drug. He brought what he thought was a prohibited drug, but was in fact a harmless substance, through customs. The House of Lords held that on the true construction of s.1 of the **Criminal Attempts Act 1981** D was guilty, even if the facts were such that it was impossible to commit the actual offence. All that was needed was an act more than merely preparatory to the commission of the offence D *intended* to commit. Such an act was present in this case. There was no clear distinguishing principle to differentiate *Anderton v Ryan*. It was clear from the Law Commission's Report on Attempt and Impossibility that the *Anderton v Ryan* situation was intended to be covered by the Act. *Anderton v Ryan* was, therefore, overruled.

The effect of *Shivpuri* is to confirm that attempting the impossible can be a crime. A defendant will be guilty of an attempt to commit a crime if he does an act which is more than merely preparatory towards that crime, even if the commission of the full offence is either factually or legally impossible for any reason. Trying to pick an empty pocket is a good example. It amounts to attempted theft. In *Jones* (2007), D sent a series of explicit text messages to someone he believed was a girl aged 12 but who was in fact a grown woman. In the messages, he arranged to meet her for the purpose of having sexual intercourse. He was convicted of attempting to intentionally cause or incite a child under 13 to engage in sexual activity, contrary to the Sexual Offences Act 2003 s.8. The Court of Appeal upheld his conviction, applying the rule in *Shivpuri*.

Excluded offences

It is not possible to attempt a conspiracy or to attempt to aid, abet, counsel or procure a criminal offence. There must also be a positive act for an attempt. Thus, it is not possible to attempt an offence which is only capable of commission by omission. Equally, as D must intend to attempt the offence, it is not possible to commit an offence which does not include intention in its mens rea. For example, it is not possible to be guilty of attempted manslaughter.

SUMMARY OF ATTEMPTS

ACTUS REUS
D must do the following:
- An act more than merely preparatory to the commission of an offence ("embarking on a crime proper" *Gullefer*).

MENS REA
D must possess the following:
- Intention to commit an offence (s.1(1) CAA 1981).

CONSPIRACY

A conspiracy is an agreement by two or more persons to commit a crime. This was previously a common law offence but is now governed by the **Criminal Law Act 1977**. There are two common law conspiracy offences which have been retained by the Act: conspiracy to defraud and conspiracy to corrupt public morals or outrage public decency. Conspiracy is, therefore, governed partly by common law but for the most part, it is governed by statute.

Statutory conspiracy
Most conspiracies to commit criminal offences fall under s.1(1) of the **Criminal Law Act 1977**.

LEGISLATION HIGHLIGHTER

Criminal Law Act 1977 s.1

(1) Subject to the following provisions of this Part of this Act, if a person agrees with any other person or persons that a course of conduct shall be pursued which, if the agreement is carried out in accordance with their intentions, either

(a) will necessarily amount to or involve the commission of any offence or offences by one or more of the parties to the agreement, or

(b) would do so but for the existence of facts which render the commission of the offence or any of the offences impossible, he is guilty of conspiracy to commit the offence or offences in question.

(2) Where liability for any offence may be incurred without knowledge on the part of the person committing it of any particular fact or circumstance necessary for the commission of the offence, a person shall nevertheless not be guilty of conspiracy to commit that offence by virtue of subsection (1) above unless he and at least one other party to the agreement intend or know that that fact or circumstance shall or will exist at the time when the conduct constituting the offence is to take place.

Actus reus of conspiracy

Agreement

There must be an *agreement* to commit the same criminal offence: *Saik* (2006). Where D agrees to commit an offence which is less serious than the offence that the others in the conspiracy agree to, there is no liability. This was the case in *Barnard* (1980) when D was acquitted of conspiracy to rob where he believed he was agreeing to commit a theft. However, this is not the case where one conspirator agrees to commit a more serious offence than his co-conspirators. In that situation he will be liable. Thus if in *Barnard*, D believed there was a conspiracy to rob when in fact the agreement was only to commit theft, he would be guilty of conspiring to steal as theft is part of the more serious offence of robbery.

The agreement continues until the substantive offence either takes place, or the agreement is abandoned. Thus, more parties can join the agreement up until that point: *DPP v Doot* (1973).

With any person or persons

A conspiracy does not require all parties to meet. Provided they all have a common purpose and each conspirator has communicated with at least one other, then a conspiracy is made out: *Scott* (1979). It is also possible to charge one person without identifying the person with whom they conspired: *Philips* (1987). The intended victim of the offence, however, cannot be a conspirator, nor can a person conspire with their spouse or civil partner, nor with a person under the age of criminal responsibility: **Criminal Law Act 1977 s.2.**

Mens rea of conspiracy

The Act makes it clear that the mens rea for conspiracy is intention only and not recklessness. What is required is knowledge or intention that the circumstance or fact which will constitute a criminal offence shall or will exist at the time of the commission of the offence. Suspicion as to the facts or circumstances will not suffice, even with respect to crimes of strict liability. Furthermore, the mens rea for the substantive offence is not sufficient for the purposes of conspiracy. The prosecution must prove an intention to carry out an agreed course of conduct, which in itself amounts to an offence: *Siracusa* (1989).

KEY CASE

SAIK (2006)

D was charged with conspiracy contrary to s.1(1) of the **Criminal Law Act 1977**, to commit the offence of money laundering by converting bank notes. The substantive offence of money laundering (in s.93(2) of the **Criminal Justice Act 1988**) required proof that the defendant knew or had reasonable grounds to suspect that the property represented the proceeds of crime. D pleaded guilty to the conspiracy charge subject to the qualification that he did not "know" but only "suspected" that the money was the proceeds of crime. The House of Lords quashed his conviction. Although suspicion that the money was the proceeds of crime would be sufficient on a charge of the substantive offence, knowledge of that fact was required for a conviction of conspiracy to commit that offence. Whenever the existence of a particular fact or circumstance is required for the commission of the substantive offence, s.1(2) requires that, to be guilty of conspiracy, the defendant must intend or know that fact or circumstance shall or will exist when the conspiracy is to be carried into effect.

It is not necessary to prove that all of the conspirators intend to see through the commission of the offence.

KEY CASE

ANDERSON (1986)

D agreed with two others to supply wire cutters to enable someone to escape from prison. A fee was to be paid for the materials. D was charged with conspiracy to effect the escape of a prisoner but argued that he had no intention to see the plan through. He simply intended to collect most of the fee and then use the money to leave the United Kingdom, playing no further part in the plan. His conviction was upheld by the House of Lords.

Interestingly, it was held obiter dicta in *Anderson* that a defendant would only be guilty of conspiracy if he planned to play some active part in the carrying out of the agreement. The ratio decidendi of the case has been ignored in later cases, including *Edwards* (1991) where the defendant had agreed to supply amphetamine and the Court of Appeal held that the trial judge had been correct in directing the jury not to convict the defendant of conspiring to supply amphetamine unless they were sure that he intended to supply it. In *Siracusa* (1989) the Court of Appeal "explained" the obiter dicta in *Anderson*, saying that there can be active or passive participation and that an intention to participate in furtherance of the crime can be established by a failure to stop the criminal acts of other conspirators.

The course of conduct must amount to a criminal offence or several offences. The offence does not have to take place in the United Kingdom. It is not possible to conspire to aid, abet, counsel or procure a criminal offence as there is no guarantee that the principal will carry out the offence so the agreement is not certain (*Kenning & Others* (2008)). Although there must be more than one person to form a conspiracy, it is only necessary that one of the co-conspirators be capable of carrying out the offence. In *Sherry* (1993), two Ds were indicted for a conspiracy to abduct the son of one of them, contrary to s.1 of the Child Abduction Act 1984. Only one of them was a specified person capable of committing the s.1 offence, but that was sufficient for the purposes of their conspiracy liability.

Conspiracy at common law

The only conspiracies left at common law are conspiracy to defraud, conspiracy to corrupt public morals and conspiracy to outrage public decency. Note that outraging public decency may well be a criminal offence in itself and therefore covered by the statutory form of the offence under s.1.

Conspiracy to defraud

Actus reus

The actus reus of conspiracy to defraud was explained by Viscount Dilhorne in *Scott v Metropolitan Police Commissioner* (1975) to be an agreement by two or more persons to deprive a person of something which is his or to which he is, or would be, entitled, by dishonesty, or to injure some proprietary right of another by dishonesty.

Scott v Metropolitan Police Commissioner (1975)

D and others agreed to copy certain films without permission and without paying fees, and to make money by showing these copies and charging for admission. There was no deception involved and, therefore, an offence under the **Theft Act 1968** was difficult to prove. The House of Lords held that this was a conspiracy to defraud and deceit was unnecessary for that offence if the plan involved the use of other dishonest means.

A conspiracy need not be such that, if carried out, it would definitely cause an individual to suffer loss. It is sufficient if it would put his economic or proprietary interests at risk: *Allsop* (1976).

Mens rea

There are two elements to the mens rea of this offence. Firstly, D must intend to defraud. Thus, his purpose must be to cause the victim economic loss. This will include the situation where D's intention is to personally gain in the knowledge that the victim will be caused a loss: *Cooke* (1986).

The second element is dishonesty. The test for dishonesty is set out in the case of *Ghosh* (1982) and involves both a subjective test and objective test. The *Ghosh* test, as it is commonly referred to, is set out in Ch.10.

Conspiracy to corrupt public morals

The common law offence has been retained by **Criminal Law Act 1977** s.5(3) which states that the offence is committed where there is an agreement to "engage in conduct which (a) tends to corrupt public morals or outrages public decency; but (b) would not amount to or involve the commission of an offence if carried out by a single person otherwise than in pursuance of an agreement".

This offence first appeared in a modern case in 1962.

Shaw v Director of Public Prosecutions (1962)

D published a "Ladies Directory" containing details of prostitutes and the sexual acts they were prepared to practise. D was charged with conspiring with the prostitutes to corrupt public morals. The House of Lords held that there was such an offence at common law, and affirmed D's conviction.

It was decided in the case of *Knuller* (1973) that corrupting public morals meant "conduct which a jury might find to be destructive of the very fabric of society" (per Lord Simon).

KEY CASE

KNULLER V DPP (1973)

D and others published advertisements in a contact magazine aimed at male homosexuals. The House of Lords held that this was a conspiracy to corrupt public morals, thus confirming that this offence did exist. However, their Lordships explained that the jury needed to be directed to consider whether the people likely to read the material were likely to be depraved and corrupted and "deprave and corrupt" were strong words meaning more than just leading morally astray. Their Lordships also firmly rejected the idea put forward in *Shaw* that the House had a residual power to create new common law offences.

Conspiracy to outrage public decency

Outraging public decency is itself an offence. Thus a conspiracy to commit it is now a statutory conspiracy under s.1. An example of such an offence is *Gibson* (1990) in which the defendant, an artist, had included in a public display of his work a pair of earrings made from freeze-dried foetuses. He was convicted of the common law offence of outraging public decency.

Conspiracy to do the impossible

Since the Criminal Law Act 1977 was amended by the **Criminal Attempts Act 1981,** the law relating to impossible conspiracies is now in line with that relating to impossible attempts. It follows that, for example, where two people agree to extract cocaine from a substance in their possession which, unknown to them, contains no cocaine, they will, despite the impossibility of achieving their objective, nevertheless be guilty of conspiring to produce a controlled drug. The leading authority on impossible attempts, *Shivpuri* (see above), can therefore be applied by analogy to impossible conspiracies. For a discussion of the different types of impossibility, see above.

SUMMARY OF CONSPIRACY

ACTUS REUS
D must do the following:
- Make an agreement.
- With any person or persons.
- To carry out a course of conduct which will amount to a criminal offence by one or more parties to the agreement.

MENS REA
D must possess the following:
- Knowledge or intention to carry out a course of conduct which amounts to an offence (*Siracusa*).

ASSISTING OR ENCOURAGING CRIME

At common law it was an offence to "incite" another person to commit an offence. Incitement was committed if D advised, encouraged, induced, threatened or pressurised another party to commit a crime, irrespective of whether the offence actually took place. The common law incitement offence has now been abolished by the Serious Crime Act 2007 and has been replaced by three new offences which involve encouraging or assisting crime. Note that a number of specific incitement offences still remain such as inciting a child to engage in sexual activity under the **Sexual Offences Act 2003** s.10, or soliciting murder under the **Offences Against the Person Act 1861** s.4.

Liability for assisting or encouraging crime is contained in the **Serious Crime Act 2007** ss.44–46. The offences are further defined and explained in ss.47-58 and ss.64-67 of the 2007 Act. In *Sadique and Hussain* (2011), the Court of Appeal acknowledged that the provisions are "very complex" but held that they are "neither vague nor uncertain". In summary the offences are as follows:

Doing an act capable of encouraging or assisting the commission of:
- an offence, with **intent** to encourage or assist (s.44)
- an offence, **believing** it will be committed and **believing** that the act will encourage or assist (s.45); or
- one or more offences, **believing** that one or more of them will be committed and **believing** that the act will encourage or assist (s.46)

For example, in *Blackshaw, Sutcliffe and Others* (2011), the defendant Sutcliffe (S) was charged with committing a s.44 offence during the 2011 riots. S created a facebook event entitled "The Warrington Riots" inviting members of the public to meet at a particular venue in Warrington. S subsequently pleaded guilty to encouraging or assisting the commission of riot. The defendant Blackshaw (B) also created a public event on facebook during the riots. B pleaded guilty to a s.46 offence on the basis that this act was capable of encouraging riot, burglary and criminal damage.

Actus reus

All three offences require the doing of an act capable of encouraging or assisting an offence, while s.46 applies if the act is capable of encouraging or assisting multiple offences.

The phrase "doing an act" is explained in s.65. Section 65(2)(a) provides that D does an act capable of encouraging or assisting an offence if he takes steps to reduce the possibility of criminal proceedings being brought in relation to that offence. Section 65(2)(b) states that doing an act includes "failing to take reasonable steps to discharge a duty". Thus, the offence can be committed either by a positive act, or by an omission. Section 67 provides that an act may take the form of a "course of conduct". The act or omission must be "capable" of encouraging or assisting another to commit a crime; it is irrelevant whether the act actually does achieve these things.

Encouraging includes (but is not limited to) doing an act which threatens another person or otherwise puts pressure on another person to commit an offence: s.65(1). While this is rather widely drafted, it follows the case law on the previous offence of incitement.

Mens rea

The mens rea for each offence is slightly different. The s.44 offence requires intention to encourage or assist the commission of an offence. This does not include the situation where encouragement or assistance was a foreseeable consequence of D's action: **Serious Crime Act 2007** s.44(1) and (2). Thus only direct intention (in the sense of D's desire or purpose) will suffice.

Section 45 requires D to: (1) believe that an offence will be committed and (2) believe that his act will encourage or assist the offence's commission: **Serious Crime Act 2007** s.47(3). Note that a belief that an offence *might* be committed, or a belief that D's act *might* encourage or assist, is not sufficient.

Section 46 requires that D believes: (1) that one or more offences will (not might) be committed (but has no belief as to which) and (2) that D's act will (not might) encourage or assist the commission of one or more of the offences. An example of this might be where D gives a knife to another, unsure of whether that person will use it to injure someone or simply threaten someone with it in a public place, the latter constituting the offence of at least possession of a bladed article in a public place. D should only be charged under s.46 where the prosecution allege that D did an act that was objectively capable of assisting more than one offence. Each of these "reference offences" must be identified and each should form the basis of a separate charge: *Saddique and Hussain*. If it becomes clear at trial that D in fact had only one offence in mind, D will nevertheless be liable under s.46: *Saddique and Hussain*.

According to s.47(5)(a), which applies to all three offences, where the offences that D is assisting or encouraging another to commit require some fault element (i.e. it is not a strict liability offence) then D must believe or be reckless as to whether the person who commits the offence will do so with the required fault. This requires D to anticipate that the other person will have the necessary mens rea for the offence that D is encouraging or assisting. Alternatively, D will be liable if his state of mind is such that, were he to commit the offence, it would be done with the required fault.

Equally s.47(5)(b) states that if the offence requires proof of particular circumstances or consequences or both, D must believe or be reckless as to whether those circumstances will be present, or the consequence achieved, should the other person actually commit the offence. This requires D to have a belief that the relevant circumstances will exist and some foresight of any relevant consequences (recklessness).

KEY CASE

SADIQUE AND HUSSAIN (2011)

D was convicted of an offence under s.46 of the **Serious Crime Act 2007** where he and others were concerned with a national distribution business supplying chemical cutting agents (e.g. benzocaine; lignocaine and other chemicals) direct to drug dealers and to regional distributors of cutting agents. The supply of the cutting agents was held to be capable of assisting one or more offences of supplying/being concerned in the supply of class A or class B controlled drugs, and D believed that one or more of those offences would be committed and that his act would assist in the commission of one or more of the said offences.

Notably, it was also held by the Court of Appeal in *Sadique and Hussain* (2011), that the s.46 offence was not incompatible with Article 7 of the European Convention on Human Rights.

Does the offence which has been encouraged or assisted have to be committed?

D is liable for encouraging or assisting a crime irrespective of whether the other person actually goes on to commit the substantive offence: s.49(1). It should be noted that offences of assisting or encouraging crime overlap quite significantly with secondary liability of aiding, abetting, counselling or procuring. Where the substantive offence has actually been committed, D may either be charged as an accessory (secondary party) or with encouraging or assisting the offence under the **Serious Crime Act 2007.**

Defence of acting reasonably

Section 59 provides a defence where D proves either: (1) that he "knew" certain circumstances existed and that it was reasonable for him to act as he did in those circumstances; or (2) that he "believed" certain circumstances existed, that the belief was reasonable, and it was reasonable for him to act as he did in the circumstances as he believed them to be. Section 59(3) provides that factors to be considered in determining whether it was reasonable for a person to act as he did include: the seriousness of the anticipated offence; any purpose for which D claims to have been acting; and any authority under which he claims to have been acting. Note that the burden of proof is borne by D, who must prove the s.59 defence on the balance of probabilities.

Impossibility and attempts

The Act makes no mention of impossibility but a literal reading of the sections would suggest that D could be liable for encouraging or assisting, even if the substantive offence is impossible. D could do an act capable of encouraging or assisting a criminal offence, even if the offence could not be committed, provided that his act was *capable* of encouraging or assisting the offence. If D's act is incapable of providing encouragement or assistance, D could not be guilty even if he intended to provide such encouragement (he might be guilty of attempting to do an act which would have been capable of encouraging or assisting). Notably however, it was not possible to be convicted of inciting the impossible under the old law, so this issue awaits a decision of the courts.

It was possible to be guilty of attempted incitement and it remains possible for D to be convicted of attempting to encourage or assist the commission of a crime under **Criminal Attempts Act 1981** s.1.

SUMMARY OF ENCOURAGING OR ASSISTING A CRIMINAL OFFENCE

Actus reus
D must do an act "capable of encouraging or assisting an offence" (s.44 & 45) or one or more of a number of offences (s.46)

Mens rea s.44	Mens rea s.45	Mens rea s.46
Intention to encourage or assist	Believing an offence will be committed AND believing that the act will encourage or assist	Believing one or more offences will be committed AND believing that the act will encourage or assist

PROPOSALS FOR REFORM

The Law Commission published a consultation paper in 2007 entitled *Conspiracy and Attempts* (Law Com. No.183) which suggested that the offence of attempt should be abolished and replaced with two new attempt offences. The first is where D reaches the last acts needed to commit the offence and the second is an offence of "criminal preparation". The Law Commission proposed that both offences would require proof that D intended to commit the substantive offence and that both offences would carry the same maximum penalty as the substantive offence. The last act test would be the same as outlined in *Eagleton*, above. This proposal was abandoned in the Law Commission's final report (Law Com. No. 318).

In relation to conspiracy, the same paper (Law Com. No. 318) suggested abolishing spousal immunity and the exemption from liability for conspiracy for the intended victim of an offence, although it was recommended that the exemption for victims should be retained, where the victim is within the category of persons the offence was designed to protect. While the recommendations were accepted, they will not be implemented.

You should now know and understand:

☐ what inchoate offences are;

☐ what constitutes a criminal attempt;

☐ what constitutes a conspiracy;

☐ what constitutes encouraging or assisting an offence.

· ·
QUESTION AND ANSWER
· ·

QUESTION

Bill is the manager of the local bank. Tom and Nigel plan to break into Bill's house one night and force him at gunpoint to open up the bank and its vault so that they can steal the money kept there. On the relevant night, Tom has second thoughts and stays at home in bed. Nigel carries out the planned offence alone.

Consider the criminal liability of Tom and Nigel in this scenario.

ADVICE AND THE ANSWER

Start by identifying the criminal offence and then ascertain what type of inchoate offence is likely to have been committed.

Answer guide:

This could be a conspiracy to burgle. Tom and Nigel have made an agreement to undertake a course of action which amounts to an offence (burglary): *Saik*. Burglary is entering a building/part of a building as a trespasser with intent to steal, commit criminal damage or commit GBH: **Theft Act 1968** s.9(1)(a) (see Ch.10).

The mens rea required is intention to carry out the agreed course of conduct which amounts to an offence: *Siracusa*. They both have this intention at the time of the agreement. Tom cannot escape liability by failing to participate. In *Siracusa* the Court of Appeal understood a failure to stop the acts of other conspirators as intention to commit the crime.

Defences

6

INTRODUCTION

Although the defendant may have committed the actus reus and mens rea of a crime, if a defence is pleaded successfully, the defendant will escape liability. Some defences can result in a complete acquittal, while others result in conviction for a lesser offence. Some defences are available to all crimes, while others are only available to certain offences.

The normal rule is that it is for the prosecution to prove that the accused is guilty and to do so beyond reasonable doubt: *Woolmington v DPP* (1935). In relation to defences, the defendant usually bears an evidential burden, meaning that he must adduce sufficient evidence for the trial judge to leave the defence to the jury. It is then for the prosecution to disprove the defence to the normal criminal standard (i.e. beyond reasonable doubt). Some defences however, reverse the burden of proof so that the defendant bears the burden of proving the elements of the defence. Where the defendant bears the burden of proof in relation to an issue, the requisite standard of proof is proof on the balance of probabilities.

This chapter will outline the elements of the main criminal defences and will identify the types of offence to which they may be pleaded. Procedural and evidential issues will also be considered in relation to each defence where relevant.

INSANITY

Insanity is also known as insane automatism. The defence of insanity relates to the mental condition of the accused. Insanity must be distinguished from *unfitness to plead*. An accused can be found unfit to plead, if *at the time of trial*, he is found to lack sufficient intellect to comprehend the course of criminal proceedings. For example, a defendant will be unfit to plead if he is incapable of understanding the charge(s) and the pleas open to him, or of following the evidence. In this case the trial will not proceed. The *defence of insanity* will arise where the accused is found to have been insane *at the time the offence was allegedly committed*. The defence will be raised at trial and, if successful, will result in a special verdict of "not guilty by reason of insanity".

In *DPP v Harper* (1997), the Divisional Court held that insanity was only available to an offence being tried in the magistrates' court if that offence required proof of mens rea (i.e. it was not available to crimes of strict liability). However, *DPP v Harper* is generally regarded as having been wrongly decided and it is thought that insanity is a general defence which is available to all crimes in both the magistrates' court and the Crown Court (*Insanity and Automatism* Law Com. Discussion Paper, 2013).

The M'Naghten Rules

The elements of the defence of insanity were set out in the *M'Naghten* Rules (1843). Daniel M'Naghten killed the prime minister's private secretary but a jury acquitted him of murder on the ground that he was insane. The *M'Naghten* Rules were laid down by a panel of judges of the House of Lords in response to questions which arose in Parliament following the not guilty verdict. The Rules state that every man is presumed to be sane unless the contrary is proved. To establish insanity the accused has to show, on a balance of probabilities, that he satisfies the following test:

CHECKPOINT

"... at the time of the committing of the act the party accused was labouring under such a defect of reason, from disease of the mind, as not to know the nature and quality of the act he was doing; or, if he did know it, that he did not know he was doing what was wrong."

Accordingly, the defendant must prove three separate elements to establish a defence of insanity:

(i) Defect of reason

D must have been "deprived of the power of reasoning" (per Ackner J. in *Clarke* (1972)).

KEY CASE

CLARKE (1972)
D was accused of theft from a shop. Her defence rested on forgetfulness due to depression. The trial judge ruled that the defence of insanity was applicable, so she changed her plea to guilty and then appealed. The Court of Appeal quashed her conviction saying that "defect of reason" required D's powers of reasoning to be impaired. A failure to use powers of reasoning due to forgetfulness was not sufficient.

Similarly, an inability to control emotions or impulses does not support a defence of insanity because it is not a defect of reason: *Kopsch* (1927).

(ii) From disease of the mind
The defect of reason must arise from a disease of the mind. The legal definition of "disease of the mind" does not necessarily coincide with the medical definition.

KEY CASE

KEMP (1957)
D suffered from arteriosclerosis which caused him to have temporary blackouts. During one of these he attacked his wife with a hammer causing her grievous bodily harm. A disease of the mind was held to be any disease affecting the ordinary mental faculties of reason, memory and understanding, including, for example, *Kemp's* arteriosclerosis. A disease of the mind can be temporary or permanent, curable or incurable.

The defence of insanity has to be distinguished from automatism. A "disease of the mind" is a condition which affects the defendant's mental faculties, whereas automatism is where the defendant was not consciously in control of his actions at the time of the offence. In order to differentiate between insanity and automatism, the courts have adopted a test which distinguishes between internal and external factors, the latter being automatism rather than insanity. A number of key cases on the subject are outlined below.

KEY CASE

QUICK (1973)
D, a diabetic, injured a person while suffering from hypoglycaemia. The trial judge ruled that D's only possible defence was insanity. D then pleaded guilty and appealed against the ruling. The Court of Appeal allowed D's appeal and held that the blackout was not caused by the disease (his diabetes), but by taking insulin and then failing to eat. The taking of the insulin was an external factor and, as the temporary effect of the application of an external factor is not a disease of the mind, the appropriate defence was automatism rather than insanity. Diabetes, however, is a disease and if it is caused a defect of reason in the absence of an external factor, that could amount to insanity.

KEY CASE

SULLIVAN (1983)
While suffering from a seizure due to psychomotor epilepsy, D kicked and injured a man. Medical evidence showed that the offence was probably committed during the third stage of the seizure, during which D would not have been aware of his bodily movements. The House of Lords held that epilepsy was a disease of the mind because D's mental faculties were impaired to the extent of causing a defect of reason. It was irrelevant that epliepsy was an organic disease which was only intermittent.

KEY CASE

HENNESSEY (1989)
D was charged with taking a conveyance without authority and driving whilst disqualified. He was a diabetic who had been suffering from stress and anxiety. He had not taken insulin or eaten for several days and the offences were committed during a state of hyperglycaemia. D claimed that he had not been in control of his actions and pleaded automatism. The trial judge ruled that, if true, this amounted to insanity. The Court of Appeal upheld the ruling, holding that the hyperglycaemia was caused by an internal condition (diabetes), which was a disease of the mind. The stress and anxiety could not be treated as external causative factors. *Quick* was distinguished because in that case D's hypoglycaemia was caused by the external factor of taking insulin and not by the diabetes itself.

Until 1991 sleepwalking was thought to be an example of automatism rather than insanity. However, the Court of Appeal now treats sleepwalking as a disease of the mind with internal causes unless there is clear evidence of an external causal factor.

KEY CASE

BURGESS (1991)
D committed an offence of violence while sleepwalking. The Court of Appeal held that the sleepwalking was caused by an internal factor and that the ordinary stresses and anxieties of life which may have triggered the sleepwalking were not sufficient to constitute an external factor. The appropriate defence was insanity.

It has long been established that a disease of the mind which is caused by intoxication, such as delirium tremens resulting from the withdrawal of alcohol, could support a defence of insanity: *Davis* (1881). However, in *Coley, McGhee and Harris* (2013), the Court of Appeal emphasised that the voluntary consumption of intoxicants is an external factor and the direct acute effects of such intoxication are not a disease of the mind.

(iii) D must not know what he was doing or must not know that what he did was wrong

Where there is a defect of reason from disease of the mind, it must be proved that either the defendant did not know the nature and quality of his act, or he did not know that his act was wrong. The former covers the rare situation where the defendant, because of a defect of reason, does not understand the physical nature and quality of his act: *Codere* (1917).

If D relies on the wrongfulness limb of the *M'Naghten* test, he must show that he did not realise that his actions were *legally* wrong. D's belief that his actions were morally right would not support the defence if he realised that what he was doing was against the law.

KEY CASE

WINDLE (1952)

D killed his wife by an overdose of aspirin. The evidence showed that, although D was suffering from a mental illness, he knew that what he was doing was against the law. The Court of Appeal affirmed his conviction on the basis that a jury cannot and should not be asked to consider whether a defendant's actions were morally right or wrong. The test is whether the defendant knew his actions were contrary to law.

Court procedure

It was accepted by the House of Lords in *Woolmington v DPP* (1935) that insanity is an exception to the usual rule that the prosecution bears the burden of disproving a defence beyond reasonable doubt. Thus, where the accused pleads insanity, it is for the accused to prove *on the balance of probabilities* that he satisfies the requirements for the defence. Medical evidence will be required to support an insanity plea.

A special verdict of not guilty by reason of insanity is not a conviction. However, under the Criminal Procedure (Insanity) Act 1964 (as amended), following a special verdict the court must make a hospital order, a supervision order or an absolute discharge. The 1964 Act, therefore, ensures that a defendant who is found to be insane will receive treatment if this is necessary.

Defendants usually prefer other mental capacity defences, such as diminished responsibility or automatism, to insanity. This may be due, at least in part, to the stigma of the label "insanity". Where a defendant raises diminished responsibility, the prosecution may argue that the appropriate defence is insanity. In that case, the burden of proof rests on the prosecution to prove insanity beyond reasonable doubt.

Proposals for reform

The *M'Naghten* Rules are almost universally regarded as unsatisfactory, and reforms have been suggested on many occasions. The Law Commission recently published a Discussion Paper on the defences of insanity and automatism. The Commission decided not to produce a formal Report on the issue as, although it was convinced that there are theoretical problems with the defences, there is little evidence that the defences cause problems in practice. The Commission's provisional proposals are discussed at p.97, below.

AUTOMATISM

Automatism applies to the rare situation where the defendant is not legally insane but is unable to control his actions for some other reason. Automatism can be regarded as as negating the mens rea because the defendant is not conscious of what he is doing. However, it is more commonly viewed as a negation of the actus reus of the offence because D's conduct is not voluntary.

The defence was described by Lord Denning in *Bratty* (1963):

CHECKPOINT

"Automatism... means an act which is done by the muscles without any control by the mind such as a spasm, a reflex action or a convulsion; or an act done by a person who is not conscious of what he is doing such as an act done whilst suffering from concussion or whilst sleepwalking." [Note that in *Burgess*, sleepwalking was held to be insanity due to the lack of external cause (see above).]

Automatism may occur, for example, when a defendant is suffering from concussion, a hypoglycaemic episode or a hypnotic trance, provided that there is an external and not an internal cause. The external factor could be a traumatic event inducing severe shock. A good example is post-traumatic stress disorder, which is increasingly being recognised by the courts.

KEY CASE

T. (1990)
A few days after having been raped, D was involved in an incident which led to charges of robbery and causing actual bodily harm. Medical evidence showed that she was suffering from post-traumatic stress disorder and was not aware of what was happening. The court held that her state of mind was caused by the external event of the rape, and it was, therefore, classed as automatism.

The requirements for the defence of automatism are a total loss of voluntary control, which is caused by an external factor. The defence will not be available if D's state of automatism was self-induced unless the offence is one of specific intent. (The distinction between crimes of specific intent and crimes of basic intent is discussed at p.82, below).

(i) Total absence of voluntary control

KEY CASE

BROOME V PERKINS (1987)
D was charged with careless driving. He suffered from diabetes and pleaded automatism on the basis that he had driven erratically due to a sudden attack of hypoglycaemia. The evidence showed that D's actions had been automatic at times, but at other times his mind was capable of controlling his limbs. The court held that, because D had been in control during at least some parts of the journey, he could not rely on the defence.

Similarly, disinhibited behaviour is not the same as behaviour over which the defendant has no voluntary control. In *Coley. McGhee and Harris* (2013), the defendant Coley (C) was charged with attempted murder. Medical evidence showed that C was detached from reality or acting under a delusion at the time of the offence. However, the Court held that C's conduct in preparing to commit the attack had been sufficiently organised for the jury to conclude that his conduct was voluntary.

(ii) Caused by an external factor

This element of the defence distinguishes automatism from insanity (see above).

(iii) Self-induced automatism

Unless the crime charged is one of specific intent, automatism is no defence if D's state was the result of the voluntary consumption of alcohol or dangerous drugs (taken otherwise than in accordance with a prescription), or if it was the result of D's recklessness. The accused will have been reckless if he recognised the risk that his behaviour (e.g. a diabetic's failure eat when taking insulin) might make him aggressive, unpredictable, or uncontrolled. Thus, if D takes soporific drugs (e.g. valium), which are not generally known to lead to such behaviour, he may rely on automatism as a defence unless he realised that the taking of the drugs might lead to such behaviour.

KEY CASE

BAILEY (1983)

D, a diabetic, attacked his ex-girlfriend's new boyfriend and injured him. D had felt unwell beforehand and had taken some sugar but no food. He suffered a hypoglycaemic episode during which he committed the assault. At trial the judge refused to allow evidence of automatism as D's state was self-induced. On appeal the Court of Appeal held that on a charge of specific intent (e.g. an offence under the **Offences Against the Person Act 1861** s.18), self-induced automatism can be a defence because it can negative the specific intent required for the offence. Further, in other crimes, it was held that self-induced automatism, other than that caused by the voluntary consumption of alcohol or drugs, can be a valid defence, unless the accused was reckless, i.e. knew that his acts or omissions (e.g. to take food) might render his conduct unpredictable, uncontrolled or aggressive.

Essentially, the rules on intoxication apply. For the rules relating to intoxication and the distinction between crimes of specific and basic intent, see below.

In *Coley, McGhee and Harris* (2013), the defendant McGhee (M) was convicted of wounding with intent, contrary to s.18 of the Offences Against the Person Act 1861. He argued that he had been in a state of automatism at the time of the offence, having consumed a combination of alcohol and temazepam (a tranquilliser). The Court of Appeal held that the defence of automatism was not available because M retained a degree of voluntary control over his actions (see above). The defence of intoxication was, therefore, the applicable defence (see below). Conversely, where intoxication did cause a total absence of control, the defence of automatism would be available.

Court procedure

If the defendant wishes to plead automatism, it is necessary for him to raise some evidence of it: *Hill v Baxter* (1958). Due to the nature of the defence, medical expert evidence will be required. A verdict of not guilty due to automatism results in an acquittal.

Automatism and insanity: a comparison

If a lack of voluntary behaviour is due to an external factor, such as medication, a blow on the head, or a traumatic event, the defence of automatism can succeed (*Quick, T*), even if the automatism is self-induced (*Bailey*). Note, however, that self-induced automatism is only a defence to crimes of specific intent. If a lack of voluntary behaviour is due to an internal factor, this will be insanity (*Sullivan, Burgess*), even if the illness or condition is temporary and curable.

Where the accused pleads automatism, the burden of disproving it (beyond reasonable doubt) lies on the prosecution. Where the accused pleads insanity, the burden of proving the defence (on a balance of probabilities) is borne by the accused. A successful plea of automatism leads to an outright acquittal, whereas a finding of not guilty by reason of insanity will result in the special verdict followed by one of the disposals outlined above.

MISTAKE

Mistake is not strictly speaking a defence. It is often considered alongside other defences as it overlaps with other defences. For example, a defendant who is raising self-defence in response to an assault charge may claim that he was mistaken as to the need to act in self-defence. This was the case in *Beckford* (1988) where D, a police officer, was charged with murder after shooting and killing a suspect. He successfully pleaded self-defence on the basis of an honest belief that the suspect was about to shoot him. The Privy Council ruled that self-defence may be established on the basis of an honest belief in the need to use force, even if that belief transpires to be mistaken.

Mistake of fact negating mens rea

An honest mistake as to the facts can negate liability if it means that the defendant lacks the necessary mens rea for the offence.

KEY CASE

MORGAN (1976)

X and friends had been drinking. X encouraged his friends to have sexual intercourse with his wife saying that she would protest but would not mean it. They did so and ignored her protests. They pleaded not guilty to rape because they claimed that they had believed that she was consenting. The House of Lords said that an honest, albeit unreasonable, belief in the victim's consent would be enough to negate liability as mens rea would be missing.

Note that the House of Lords in fact dismissed the appeal, because their Lordships were satisfied that the jury did not believe that the accused had made the mistake that they claimed to have made. [Since the decision in *Morgan*, the definition of rape has been altered so that now a mistaken belief that the victim is consenting will be defence only if it is a reasonable mistaken belief: **Sexual Offences Act 2003** s.1(1).]

If no mens rea is required with regard to one element of the actus reus (i.e. the offence is one of strict or absolute liability), then a mistake with regard to that element of the offence will not negate liability: *Bowsher* (1973).

A mistake of fact due to voluntary intoxication will not negate mens rea unless the offence with which the defendant is charged is one of specific intent. In this situation the rules on intoxication apply (see p.81, below).

Mistake of fact giving rise to a defence

In relation to self-defence and the prevention of crime, a defendant will be judged on the basis of the facts as he believed them to be.

KEY CASE

WILLIAMS (GLADSTONE) (1983)

D mistook his victim for a mugger attacking a youth and fought him off. His victim was in fact a passer-by trying to arrest the youth who had attacked and robbed a woman. D was charged with assault occasioning actual bodily harm. He claimed that he had honestly believed his victim was assaulting the youth and that he had been entitled to use reasonable force to prevent the crime occurring. On appeal D's conviction was quashed on the ground that D should be judged according to his mistaken belief as to the facts, even if his mistake was unreasonable.

It is important to remember that, in relation to self-defence and the prevention of crime there is still a requirement of reasonableness as regards the amount of force used. An accused can rely upon an unreasonable mistake as to when he can defend himself, e.g. in unreasonably thinking himself to be under attack, or in thinking himself to be under a more serious attack than he is actually under. However, he is still entitled to use only *reasonable* force, i.e. such force as is reasonably necessary to defend himself from that perceived attack.

A defendant cannot rely on self-defence or prevention of crime where voluntary intoxication causes him to make a mistake about the need to use force: s.76 Criminal Justice and Immigration Act 2008 (CJIA 2008) (see below).

Mistake of law
Ignorance of the criminal law is no excuse. Thus, it will not be a defence for the defendant who committed the actus reus of an offence, with the required mens rea, to say that he did not know that his conduct constituted a crime.

. . . .

INTOXICATION

Unless the offence is one of strict liability, a defendant will only be guilty if he possesses mens rea at the time of committing the actus reus. A defendant may claim that he lacked mens rea because he was so intoxicated as a result of consuming alcohol or other drugs that he did not know what he was doing. In some circumstances this will afford him a defence. However, the courts have developed rules which mean that a defendant who lacks mens rea due to intoxication will not necessarily be able to avoid liability.

Although intoxication is often referred to as a defence, strictly speaking it is not a defence at all. Intoxication can only ever be relevant if it causes D to lack mens rea. Thus, if an intoxicated defendant brings about the actus reus of a crime with the required mens rea, he will be liable (subject to any other defences). This is so even if he only formed mens rea because he had taken alcohol or other drugs. The phrase "a drunken intent is still an intent" is often used to encapsulate this principle: *Sheehan & Moore* (1975).

KEY CASE

KINGSTON (1994)
D committed indecent assault on a 15-year-old boy while involuntarily intoxicated. D, who had paedophiliac tendencies that were normally under control, claimed that he had been drugged by another man and

> put in a room with the boy. The other man then took photographs of D with the boy, intending to use them to blackmail D. The House of Lords confirmed D's conviction, ruling that the absence of moral fault, or reduced moral fault was irrelevant to liability. D formed the mens rea for the offence and was, therefore, guilty.

This means that intoxication will never be relevant if the crime is one of strict liability because such offences do not require mens rea (see *Carroll v DPP* (2009)). In other cases, a defendant who lacks mens rea due to involuntary intoxication will not be liable. Where a defendant lacks mens rea due to voluntary intoxication, however, he will not be guilty of a crime of specific intent but will be guilty if the crime is one of basic intent.

Voluntary intoxication

KEY CASE

The leading case on intoxication is **DPP v MAJEWSKI** (1976). D was convicted of various offences of assault. He argued that all of the offences were committed while he was so intoxicated that he did not know what he was doing. The House of Lords upheld D's convictions and ruled that evidence of voluntary intoxication cannot negative mens rea in a crime of basic intent. The effect of the House of Lords decision is that voluntary intoxication may negative mens rea in all crimes of specific intent but will not do so for any crimes of basic intent. The distinction between crimes of specific intent and crimes of basic intent is, therefore, crucial.

Crimes of basic and specific intent

Generally speaking, crimes of specific intent are crimes which require proof of an intention, whereas other crimes, including those where the mens rea is satisfied by proof of recklessness, are crimes of basic intent. Thus, murder and all attempted crimes are crimes of specific intent. Theft requires intent to permanently deprive another person of his property and is, therefore, a crime of specific intent. Another example of a specific intent crime is wounding or causing grievous bodily harm *with intent*, contrary to s.18 of the **Offences Against the Person Act 1861**. Conversely, s.20 wounding or inflicting grievous bodily harm, which requires intention *or recklessness* as to some harm, is a basic intent offence.

However, this approach does not always enable us to correctly identify specific intent offences. The courts have sometimes held that offences which require proof of an intention are crimes of basic intent. For example, in *Heard*

(2007) (see below), the Court of Appeal held that sexual assault, which requires proof of an intentional touching, was a crime of basic intent.

Ultimately, the only way to know which crimes are in which category is to look at decisions the courts have made about individual offences. On this basis, crimes of specific intent include: attempts; murder; theft; most forms of burglary; and wounding with intent. Examples of crimes of basic intent are: common assault; assault occasioning actual bodily harm; malicious wounding or inflicting grievous bodily harm contrary to s.20 of the **Offences Against the Person Act 1861**; rape; taking a conveyance without the consent of the owner; reckless criminal damage; and involuntary manslaughter. (The courts have not yet decided whether the aggravated offence of reckless arson is an offence of specific intent or an offence of basic intent: *Coley, McGhee and Harris* (2013)).

KEY CASE

In **HEARD** (2007), D, while drunk, undid his trousers, took his penis in his hand and rubbed it up and down the thigh of a police constable. He was charged with sexual assault contrary to s.3 of the Sexual Offences Act 2003, (definition in Ch.8). One of the requirements of that offence is that the defendant "intentionally touches another person". D was convicted and appealed arguing that the jury should have been directed to consider whether his drunkenness meant that he did not intend to touch the constable. The Court of Appeal observed that D clearly did intend to touch the police officer but held that D would be liable even if he had not formed the required intent because sexual assault is a crime of basic intent.

Public policy

Majewski is based on public policy considerations and is difficult to explain in logical legal terms. It is based firmly on the notion that a person who voluntarily takes alcohol or dangerous drugs should be answerable criminally for any injuries he causes while in that condition. It was suggested in *Majewski* that the taking of alcohol or drugs is itself a reckless course of conduct and this recklessness provides the mens rea for a crime of basic intent. Thus, in a crime of basic intent, if D was voluntarily intoxicated, it does not have to be proved that he actually had the mens rea. Instead, the test is whether he would have foreseen the relevant risk if he had been sober: *Richardson and Irwin* (1999).

Non-dangerous drugs

The same rules do not apply in the case of soporific drugs, which are not generally known to have, and not known to the accused to have, the potential to cause violent, aggressive or unpredictable behaviour. This is so, even if the drug was not prescribed to the defendant. In such a case D's intoxication is not itself a defence but it is relevant when the jury come to consider whether the accused was reckless.

In *Hardie* (1984), D quarrelled with the woman he was living with and took some of her valium tablets to calm himself down. While under the influence of the drugs he set fire to their flat. His defence to a charge of arson with intent to endanger life, or being reckless as to endangering life, was that he lacked mens rea due to the effect of the valium. On appeal against conviction, the Court of Appeal held that the usual rules regarding intoxication as a defence did not apply where the normal effect of the drug was soporific. Instead the jury should have been left to consider whether the defendant was reckless in taking the drug. See also *Bailey* (1983) and *Coley, McGhee and Harris* (2013) under Automatism above.

Dutch courage

Different rules also apply if the defendant deliberately gets himself intoxicated in order to give himself the courage to commit an offence. In these circumstances, if D subsequently commits the actus reus while intoxicated, he will be unable to claim lack of intent, even if the crime is one of specific intent. For example, in *Attorney General for Northern Ireland v Gallagher* (1961), D decided to kill his wife. He drank a bottle of whisky to give himself Dutch courage, before killing her with a knife. The House of Lords held that D was guilty of murder and could not rely on any lack of intent due to voluntary intoxication.

Involuntary intoxication

Involuntary intoxication is defined narrowly.

> **KEY CASE**
>
> In **ALLEN** (1988), D was given some homemade wine by one of his work colleagues. D believed that the wine had a low alcohol content when, in fact, it was extremely potent. The Court of Appeal ruled that D's subsequent intoxication was voluntary: *"Where an accused knows that he is drinking alcohol, such drinking does not become involuntary for the reason alone that he may not know the precise nature or strength of the alcohol that he is consuming."*

In *Coley, McGhee and Harris* (2013), the defendant McGhee suffered from a serious medical condition and felt compelled to consume alcohol because it helped to alleviate his symptoms. The trial judge ruled that M's intoxication was, nevertheless, voluntary and this ruling was not challenged on appeal. Thus, involuntary intoxication is limited to cases involving "spiked" drinks, or other situations in which the defendant is not aware that he is consuming intoxicants.

Where a defendant is *involuntarily* intoxicated, the rule in *Majewski* does not apply. Thus, even where the crime charged is one of basic intent, the accused can escape liability if he lacked the mens rea for the crime as a result of involuntary intoxication. However, if D does have mens rea he will be liable, even if his intoxication is entirely involuntary and blameless: *Kingston* (1994) (see above).

Intoxication and defences

D may be able to claim that he acted in self-defence, or to prevent crime, if the force that he used was reasonable in the circumstances as he believed them to be. D can rely upon these defences even if his belief was mistaken, provided that it was honestly held. However, D cannot rely on a mistaken belief in the need to use force if his mistake was attributable to voluntary intoxication.

LEGISLATION HIGHLIGHTER

Section 76(5) of the CJIA 2008 provides that a defendant cannot rely on any mistaken belief attributable to intoxication that was voluntarily induced.

Section 76(5) confirms the common law position. In *O'Grady* (1987), D fought with his friend and killed him. D was convicted of manslaughter and appealed against his conviction on the grounds that the judge had mis-directed the jury concerning self-defence. The Court of Appeal held that even if D mistakenly believed that his friend was attacking him, D could not rely on self-defence as his mistake was caused by voluntary intoxication. This position was confirmed in the later cases of *O'Connor* (1991) and *Hatton* (2005).

Conversely, in the context of statutory defences under the **Criminal Damage Act 1971**, the courts have held that a defendant can rely on an intoxicated mistake to support his defence.

KEY CASE

In **JAGGARD V DICKINSON** (1981), D was convicted of criminal damage after breaking into a house in the mistaken belief that it belonged to her friend. D's friend had given her permission to treat his house as her own. D therefore relied on the statutory defence of belief in consent under s.5(2) of the **Criminal Damage Act 1971**. The Divisional Court held that because the test in s.5(2) is specifically set out in subjective terms, D could rely on her mistaken belief even though her mistake was a result of her intoxicated state. Thus, D's appeal against conviction was allowed and her conviction was quashed. This case is relevant only to the specific defence of lawful excuse under the 1971 Act and has no wider application.

SELF-DEFENCE (PRIVATE DEFENCE)

Self-defence is often referred to as private defence as it covers defence of oneself and others, defence of property, preventing crime and assisting lawful arrest. D has a defence if he uses **reasonable force** in any of the above situations. Self-defence (including defence of another) and the defence of property are common law defences. There is a separate statutory defence under s.3(1) of the Criminal Law Act 1967, which allows the use of reasonable force in the prevention of crime or in effecting, or assisting in, a lawful arrest. The common law defences of self-defence and defence of property may overlap with the statutory defence of prevention of crime; a person who uses force to protect himself from an attack is both defending himself and preventing an offence of battery. Although the above defences are general defences, they are most commonly relied upon by defendants charged with non-fatal assaults or homicide.

D will have a defence at common law or under s.3(1) of the CLA 1967 if he used reasonable force. This requires consideration of whether it was *necessary* to use force as well as whether the *amount* of force was reasonable in the circumstances: *Palmer v R* (1971). The defence will succeed if D used such force as was (objectively) reasonable in the circumstances as he (subjectively) believed them to be: *Williams* (1987); *Owino* (1996). The following discussion focuses on self-defence but the same principles apply to defence of property and the statutory defence under s.3(1) CLA 1967. The scope of the defences was clarified by s.76 of the Criminal Justice and Immigration Act 2008 and reference is made below to the provisions of s.76 where applicable.

(i) Force used must be necessary

D must have believed that the use of force was necessary, for example to defend himself from an attack. All that is required is an honest belief in the need to use force. Section 76(4) of the CJIA 2008 confirms the common law position set out in *Williams* (1987) and *Owino* (1996): the reasonableness or otherwise of D's belief in the need to use force is relevant to whether he genuinely held that belief but, if he did, he is entitled to rely on it. If D mistakenly believed himself to be under attack, or to have been under an attack more serious than it really was, then he is judged on the facts as he believed them to be, even if his mistake was an unreasonable one: *Beckford* (1988) above. However, D cannot rely on such a mistake if the mistake was induced by voluntarily intoxication: *O'Grady* (1987); s.76(5) CJIA 2008.

D is entitled to use force in response to an apprehended assault and does not have to wait until he is attacked: *Beckford v R* (1988); *DPP v Bailey* (1995). Again, this requires an honest rather than a reasonable belief.

There was once a duty to retreat as far as possible before resorting to violence but such a duty no longer exists. The possibility that D could have retreated is merely a factor to be taken into account in deciding whether it was necessary to use force: *Bird* (1985); s.76(6A) CJIA 2008.

KEY CASE

BIRD (1985)
D had been slapped and pushed by a man. She was holding a glass in her hand at the time and she hit out at the man in self-defence without realising that she still held the glass. The trial judge directed the jury that self-defence was only available if the defendant had first shown an unwillingness to fight. The Court of Appeal quashed D's conviction and held that it was unnecessary for a defendant to demonstrate unwillingness to fight; there were circumstances where D might reasonably react immediately and without first retreating. Whether it was reasonable for D to use force is for the jury to decide on the facts of the case.

Where D acts in retaliation or to exact revenge, this will not constitute necessary force: *Hussain* (2010). However, the fact that D was the initial aggressor does not mean that self-defence is unavailable: *Rashford* (2005). D may rely on self-defence if "the tables had been turned": *Harvey* (2009), or "[i]f the violence offered by the victim was so out of proportion to what the original aggressor did that in effect the roles were reversed": *Keane* (2010).

(ii) D must use reasonable force

A person can use only such force as is reasonable in all the circumstances, and it is up to the jury to decide whether the force used was objectively reasonable. The jury must put themselves in the circumstances as D perceived them to be. Someone acting in self-defence will often be doing so in the immediacy of an attack and without having time to "weigh things to a nicety". If in such a situation, the accused did what he honestly and instinctively thought was necessary, that is most potent evidence that the accused used only such force as was reasonably necessary: *Palmer* (1971); s.76(7) CJIA 2008.

Although the accused is entitled to be judged on the facts as he believed them to be (unless it was a drunken mistake), he is not the arbiter of how much force it was reasonable to use in those circumstances. The test as to how much force is reasonable is an objective one for the jury to determine. The accused is not allowed to use as much force as *he* thought reasonably necessary. The question is whether he used more force than *the jury* considers was reasonably necessary to defend himself: *Owino* (1996). In determining this question, a jury is not entitled to take into account psychiatric evidence about the defendant's mental state: *Martin (Anthony)* (2001); *Oye* (2013).

KEY CASE

MARTIN (ANTHONY) (2001)

D was being burgled by two people. He shot them, killing one. Rejecting his defence of self-defence, the jury convicted him of murder. D appealed, arguing that new evidence (that he had been suffering from a paranoid personality disorder) was relevant to the issue of whether the force used was reasonable. The Court of Appeal held that evidence of a defendant's psychiatric condition is not relevant to the issue of reasonable force, other than in exceptional circumstances making such evidence especially probative. The court did, however, reduce D's conviction from murder to manslaughter by reason of diminished responsibility.

(iii) The force used must be proportionate

Except in householder cases (see below), s.76(6) of the CJIA 2008 provides that the degree of force is not to be regarded as reasonable if it was disproportionate in the circumstances as D believed them to be.

(iv) Householder cases

In 2010, the Government's Coalition Agreement promised to "ensure that people have the protection that they need when they defend themselves against intruders". Accordingly, s.76 of the CJIA 2008 was amended. Section 76(5A) now provides that the amount of force used by a householder on an intruder does not have to be proportionate in the circumstances as the householder believes them to be. As long as the amount of force used is not "grossly disproportionate", the jury may consider it to be reasonable.

Court procedure

If the issue of self-defence is raised, the burden of proof rests on the prosecution. Thus, the accused is entitled to be acquitted unless the prosecution prove beyond all reasonable doubt that he was not acting in self-defence or that he used more than reasonable force.

The judge does not, however, have to direct the jury on the issue of self-defence unless that issue is raised or there is some evidence on which it could be raised.

The defence operates as an "all or nothing" defence; therefore, if successful it will result in the acquittal of the accused, even if the charge is one of murder. On a murder charge, a finding that the accused acted in self-defence but used excessive force means that the defence must fail but it does *not* result in a lowering of the verdict to manslaughter. The verdict may be reduced from murder to manslaughter on *other* grounds, such as loss of self control or lack of proof that the accused intended to kill or cause grievous bodily harm.

KEY CASE

MCINNES (1971)

D was involved in a fight between two rival gangs. He had a knife and claimed (at his later trial for murder) that his victim ran on to it. He appealed against his conviction for murder arguing that the judge's direction on self-defence was wrong in law. Dismissing the appeal, the Court of Appeal held that there was no provision for murder to be reduced to manslaughter on the grounds that the accused had acted in self-defence but had used excessive force. The court pointed out the possibility of provocation reducing murder to manslaughter. The court also confirmed that there is no rule that for a successful plea of self-defence the defendant must have retreated. The possibility of him retreating is simply a factor for the jury to take into account in deciding whether the accused used more force than was reasonably necessary.

CLEGG (1995)

D, a soldier, had fired at a stolen car being driven past him at a check point and killed a passenger. The House of Lords confirmed his conviction for murder because the trial judge had found as a question of fact that the amount of force used was unreasonable and excessive. Their Lordships confirmed the law established in *McInnes* and refused to bring about any change in the law by introducing a partial defence of self-defence reducing liability to manslaughter, saying that that was a job for Parliament and not the courts, however desirable the change might be. [For the Law Commission's proposed reform of the law, see below.]

CONSENT

For the purposes of the defence of consent, crimes can be divided into two categories: (i) sexual offences, such as rape and sexual assault, where the consent of the victim means that the actus reus of the offence is not complete; (ii) offences against the person, where the presence of consent may mean that the force or harm was not unlawful. Consent in the context of sexual offences is dealt with in Ch. 8. Consent as a defence to offences of violence is explained in Ch. 7. Note that there are some crimes within the above two categories, such as murder and offences involving sexual activity with a child under 16, to which consent is not available as a defence.

DURESS

Duress covers the situation where the defendant is forced to break the law because of threats towards him or another person close to him. He will, therefore, fully accept committing both the actus reus and mens rea of an offence but is excusing his behaviour on the grounds that he was compelled to act as he did. It is a general defence available to all crimes with the exception of murder, attempted murder and, possibly treason. The general rationale of the defence is that the criminal law should not demand a standard of resistance to threats which an ordinary reasonable person would find irresistible.

There are two types of duress: duress by threats and duress of circumstances (sometimes referred to as the defence of "necessity", see below). In duress by threats, the defendant will be subjected to some threats by another person forcing him to commit a criminal offence. In duress of circumstances, the threats will not come from a person but from the circumstances that the defendant finds himself in. The rules are the same for both.

Requirements of the defence of duress

The requirements for the defence were confirmed by the House of Lords in *Hasan* (2005).

(i) Threat of death or serious injury

The defendant must either be threatened with death or serious injury or, in a case of duress of circumstances, the circumstances must cause D to fear death or serious injury. In *Aikens* (2003), the court doubted that a threat to punch D would suffice. Nor is psychological injury sufficient: *Baker and Wilkins* (1997).

(ii) Directed against D or someone for whom D reasonably regards himself as responsible

The threats may be made towards D personally, or towards a member of D's family, or towards a person for whom D reasonably feels responsible. In *Ortiz* (1986) D was forced into taking part in a cocaine smuggling operation after being told that if he refused his wife and children would disappear. D pleaded duress at trial but this was rejected by the jury. The Court of Appeal, however, stated that a threat towards others was within the scope of the defence.

(iii) Reasonable belief and a good cause to fear

The jury must consider whether D was, or may have been, compelled to act as he did because, as a result of what he reasonably believed to be the situation, he had good cause to fear that otherwise death or serious injury would result. The jury must also consider whether a sober person of reasonable firmness possessing D's characteristics might have acted in the same or a similar way to D. The defence will fail if a sober person of reasonable firmness would have resisted the threats.

The reasonable man shares some of the characteristics of D. These characteristics can include the age and sex of the accused, pregnancy and serious physical disability: *Bowen* (1997). Drug addiction, however, is a self-induced condition, not a characteristic: *Flatt* (1996). Although evidence of an underlying psychiatric illness or mental impairment may be relevant according to *Antar* (2004), it is not a relevant characteristic that the accused was "extra pliable" or vulnerable to pressure: *Horne* (1994). In *Hegarty* (1994), D committed a robbery and claimed to have been subject to duress from persons who had threatened his family. He wanted to introduce medical evidence of his emotional instability and neurosis to show that he was particularly vulnerable to threats. The Court of Appeal held that emotional instability was not a relevant characteristic.

(iv) Causal effect of the threat

The offence must be directly caused by the threats or circumstances, although they do not have to be the sole factors operating on D's mind: *Valderama Vega* (1985).

KEY CASE

COLE (1994)

Moneylenders threatened "unpleasant consequences" to D unless he repaid his debt. In order to get the money he robbed a building society. The court recognised that there were two versions of duress: duress by threats and duress of circumstances. Denying him the defence on both versions, the court held that there must be a connection between the threat and the crime committed. Here there was no causal connection because those making the threats had not nominated the crime to be committed. (The defence of duress also failed in this case because the execution of the threat was not sufficiently imminent, see below).

(v) Immediacy of the threat

Execution of the threat must be imminent, which means "immediate or almost immediate" (*Hasan*). An opportunity to take evasive action, for example by contacting the police, may prevent the defence from being successful.

KEY CASE

HUDSON V TAYLOR (1971)

Two teenage girls committed perjury after having been threatened that, if they told the truth to the court, they would be "cut up". The Court of Appeal held that the threat had been sufficiently immediate to support a defence of duress, as their "duressor" had been present in court when they gave evidence and the threat could easily have been carried out on the streets of their hometown that evening. Doubt was cast upon this decision by Lord Bingham in *Hasan* (below). If the threat is not one which the defendant reasonably expects to be carried out immediately or almost immediately, the jury is likely to find that the defendant could have avoided committing the crime by going to the police or taking other evasive action.

A delay in alerting the police does not necessarily mean that the defence will fail. In *Pommell* (1995), D was charged with having possession of a firearm without a licence. He claimed that a man had visited him at 1a.m. carrying a loaded gun with the intention of using it to shoot some people later on. D said that he persuaded the man to leave the gun with D. The police had found D in possession of the gun at 8a.m. the same morning when executing a search warrant at D's premises. The Court of Appeal held that, assuming D's account was (or might be) true, D could rely upon the defence of duress for his initial possession of the gun. Whether that defence was available to a charge arising out of his continued possession of the weapon until 8a.m. depended on whether the jury considered that, in not contacting the police earlier, he had failed to desist from committing the crime as soon as he reasonably could.

(vi) Voluntary exposure to duress

Where D voluntarily associates with criminals or voluntarily joins a violent criminal gang, whose members later exercise duress upon D to compel D to commit an offence, duress will fail if D foresaw, or ought to have foreseen, the risk of being subjected to threats of violence.

KEY CASE

Hasan (2005)

D was a driver and minder for a woman who was involved in prostitution. The woman's boyfriend (F), who also acted as her minder, was involved in illegal drugs and had a reputation for violence. D carried out an armed burglary. When charged with aggravated burglary, D claimed that F had threatened him with death or serious injury. The judge directed the jury that D's defence of duress would fail if the jury found that, by associating with F, D had voluntarily exposed himself to the risk of being subjected to threats. In a wide review of the defence of duress, the House of Lords observed that duress is a defence that is easily pleaded and peculiarly difficult for the prosecution to disprove beyond all reasonable doubt. Where policy decisions had to be made, their Lordships were inclined to tighten rather than relax the conditions required for the defence to succeed.

In *Hasan*, their Lordships held that the defence of duress is excluded when the defendant foresaw, or ought reasonably to have foreseen, the risk of being subjected to any compulsion by threats of violence as a result of voluntarily associating with others engaged in criminal activity.

Mistake as to duress

Where D claims that he believed, albeit mistakenly, that he was under duress or that the threats being applied were more serious than they really were, he can rely only upon what he *reasonably* believed to be the situation. That rule, stated by the Court of Appeal in *Graham* (1982) and confirmed by the House of Lords in *Howe* (1986), was re-confirmed by Lord Bingham in *Hasan*.

Duress as a defence to murder

Duress is no defence to murder or attempted murder. That is so irrespective of whether the defendant is alleged to be the principal offender or a secondary party.

KEY CASE

HOWE (1986)

D and another person were involved in one murder as secondary parties. They were also principals to another murder and had conspired to kill a third person. They put forward duress as a defence, were convicted and appealed. It was held in the House of Lords that duress is no defence to murder when the accused is charged as principal offender. Their Lordships held that, equally, duress was no defence to someone charged with murder as a secondary party, thereby reversing the earlier decision of the House of Lords in *Lynch* (1975).

KEY CASE

GOTTS (1992)

D attempted to murder his mother. His father had threatened to shoot him unless he did so. D's appeal against his conviction failed. The House of Lords held that duress is no defence to attempted murder.

One difficulty with the decisions in *Howe* and *Gotts* is that whether a defence is available to an offender who commits an act of serious violence is, to some extent, a matter of chance. D may, for example, be scared by threats into inflicting violence with intent to cause grievous bodily harm. If D's actions result in the victim's death, D has no defence of duress and is guilty of murder. If D's actions result in grievous bodily harm, the defence of duress is available. The Law Commission has recommended allowing duress as a defence to murder and attempted murder to avoid such anomalous results (see below).

Court procedure

Duress is a complete defence. The accused may have committed the actus reus and had the mens rea for the crime charged but, if the requirements set out above are satisfied, the defence succeeds and results in an acquittal. Once duress is raised, it is for the prosecution to establish beyond all reasonable doubt that at least one of the requirements is not satisfied.

NECESSITY

Duress of circumstances has in the past sometimes been characterised as "necessity". For example, prison officers were entitled to force feed prisoners in order to save their lives in the case of *Leigh v Gladstone* (1909). A doctor was entitled to carry out abortion for the purpose of saving the life of the mother in the case of *Bourne* (1939).

In more recent times the "necessity" label has been used to describe, for example, the situation where someone seizes another and forcibly drags him from the path of an oncoming vehicle, thereby saving him from injury or even death: per Lord Goff in *Re F* (1990). It may be that all these examples are really cases of a defence of necessity distinct from the defence of duress, since they are not cases of a defendant's will being overborne. Instead they are situations where the circumstances were so compelling that the defendant felt, and most normal people would feel, that he ought to act the way he did. Even before the defence of duress was judicially recognised, the courts had been reluctant to allow the defence of necessity to a charge of murder.

> ### KEY CASE
>
> #### DUDLEY AND STEPHENS (1884)
> Ds, after being ship-wrecked and without food and water for several days, killed and ate a third member of their crew. They were convicted of murder, although the death sentence was subsequently commuted to six months' imprisonment. The judgment denied the defence of necessity. For Lord Coleridge C.J., if there was to be such a defence, it would be impossible to choose which of the crew was to die: "Who is to be the judge of this sort of necessity? By what value is the comparative value of lives to be measured?" Furthermore, the defence "once admitted might be made the legal cloak for unbridled passion and atrocious crime".

Where, however, fate has already "designated" one individual for death, the defence may be allowed, for example where D is roped to a climber who has fallen, who D cannot rescue and who, unless D cuts the rope, will pull D to his death.

Requirements for the defence

In *Re A* (2000), it was suggested that there are three requirements for the defence of necessity to succeed:

(i)   the act must be needed to avoid inevitable and irreparable evil;

(ii) no more should be done than is reasonably necessary for the purpose to be achieved; and

(iii) the evil inflicted must not be disproportionate to the evil avoided.

Note that *Re A* was a civil case and, as such, is not binding on the criminal courts although it is persuasive.

KEY CASE

RE A (CONJOINED TWINS; SURGICAL SEPARATION) (2000)

M and J were conjoined twin babies. J was capable of independent existence but M was not. M was alive only because a common artery enabled J to circulate oxygenated blood for them both. If there was no operation to separate them, both would die, probably within three to six months. If there was an operation, it would enable J to lead a normal life but would inevitably result in the death of M. The parents wished there to be no such operation. The hospital authorities approached the Court of Appeal (Civil Division) for a declaration that the operation would be lawful. It was held that the operation would be lawful and this justification came from the necessity defence:

(a)   the doctors owed conflicting duties to J (to carry out the operation to preserve her life) and to M (not to kill her) and the law had to resolve that conflict by allowing the lesser of two evils;

(b)   since M was draining J's life-blood, killing M was justified by a defence of "quasi" self-defence;

(c)   the three requirements for the defence of necessity were satisfied.

However, in *R (Nicklinson) v Ministry of Justice* (2013), the Court of Appeal held that *Re A* should be confined to its facts and that there is no general defence of necessity in the criminal law.

NICKLINSON V MINISTRY OF JUSTICE

Tony Nicklinson suffered from "locked in syndrome". He was seriously physically disabled but his mental abilities were unimpaired. He wanted to be able to choose to end his life but his condition meant that he was unable to commit suicide. He sought a declaration from the court that the common law defence of necessity was available to a charge of murder so that anyone who ended his life at his request could not be prosecuted. The Court of Appeal held that *Re A* was an exceptional case which did not have wider significance. It was not appropriate for the courts to develop a defence of necessity; the creation of a defence of necessity was a matter for Parliament.

PROPOSALS FOR REFORM

The Law Commission has published several papers containing proposals for reform of criminal defences.

Insanity and automatism

The Law Commission's Discussion Paper, *Insanity and Automatism* (2013), contains provisional proposals for the reform of both defences. The Commission proposes replacing insanity with a new defence of "not criminally responsible by reason of recognised medical condition". This defence would succeed if D could not have avoided committing the crime due to a recognised medical condition, which could be a mental or physical disorder. The defence would only be available where D totally lacked the capacity to: form a rational judgment; understand the (legal or moral) wrongfulness of his actions; or control his physical acts. The Paper also proposes reforms to the defence of automatism to ensure that it is only available where D suffers a total lack of capacity to control his actions, which is not due to a recognised medical condition. Neither of the proposed defences would be available if D's condition was self-induced.

Intoxication

The Law Commission's Report No. 229 (1995), *Intoxication and Criminal Liability,* recommends no newly created defence, but a codification of existing law, based on *Majewski*. This is seen as the most practical and workable of a variety of solutions considered. The same principle would govern voluntarily induced automatism.

Duress by threats and duress of circumstances

The Law Commission Report No. 218 (1993), *Offences Against the Person and General Principles,* recommends that duress, both by threats and of circumstances, be extended to all crimes (including murder) but that the burden of proof is shifted to D to prove his defence on a balance of probabilities. He would not have a defence if he had knowingly or unreasonably exposed himself to the risk of the threat. See also the Law Commission Report No.304 (2006), *Murder, Manslaughter and Infanticide,* p.154 below.

The justifiable use of force

The Report's recommendations on private defence would allow D to use such force as is reasonable in the circumstances as he believes them to be, but he would not be able to rely on any circumstances of which he was unaware. The Report lists the instances where the use of force would be deemed to be in public or private defence.

REVISION CHECKLIST

You should now know and understand:

☐ the defences of automatism and insanity;

☐ the defences of consent, mistake and self-defence;

☐ the defences of duress by threats, duress of circumstances and necessity;

☐ how each of the defences operates in the courts and the outcome where each defence is successful;

☐ any differences to the burden and standard of proof for each defence;

☐ the offences to which each defence can be pleaded.

Non-fatal violence offences

INTRODUCTION

The main non-fatal violence offences are common law assault and battery and the assault offences under the **Offences Against the Person Act 1861** s.47 (assault occasioning actual bodily harm), s.20 (wounding or inflicting grievous bodily harm) and s.18 (wounding or causing grievous bodily harm with intent). This chapter will consider each of these offences in turn.

ASSAULT AND BATTERY (COMMON ASSAULT)

KEY CASE

COLLINS V WILCOCK (1984)
"The law draws a distinction... between an assault and a battery. An assault is an act which causes another person to apprehend the infliction of immediate, unlawful, force on his person; a battery is the infliction of unlawful force on another person."

The term "common assault" can be used to mean either an assault or a battery. In criminal law, as in civil law, assault and battery mean different things; *Nelson* (2013), although the word "assault" is sometimes used to cover both; *Fagan v Metropolitan Police Commissioner* (1969). Although assault and battery are common law offences they are charged under s.39 of the Criminal Justice Act 2003.

LEGISLATION HIGHLIGHTER

Section 39 of the Criminal Justice Act 1988

"Common assault and battery shall be summary offences and a person guilty of either of them shall be liable to a fine not exceeding level 5 on the sliding scale, to imprisonment for a term not exceeding 6 months, or to both."

ASSAULT

Actus reus of assault

The essence of assault is that the victim is put in fear. The actus reus of assault can be committed by acts or words or a combination of both. It is now established that words alone can give rise to an assault. The House of Lords held that even the making of silent telephone calls is capable of amounting to an assault: *Ireland, Burstow* (1997) (below). Whether it is the words or acts of the defendant or a combination of both which are in issue, there will be no assault unless they cause the victim to apprehend the immediate infliction of violence. A threatening gesture which the victim does not observe cannot be an assault upon him. On the other hand, the victim does not have to be sure that violence will definitely be inflicted or that it will definitely be inflicted immediately. It is enough that the victim apprehends that it *might* be inflicted and that it *might* be inflicted immediately.

KEY CASE

CONSTANZA (1997)

D stalked his victim over a period of two years. He followed her home from work, made numerous silent telephone calls, sent over 800 letters, visited against her express wish and wrote offensive words on her front door. He sent her two letters which she interpreted as threats. She believed that he might do something to her at any time and was diagnosed as suffering from clinical depression. He appealed against his conviction for an assault occasioning actual bodily harm, arguing that there had been no assault (a) because a victim can have no fear of immediate violence unless the victim can see the alleged assailant, and (b) an assault cannot be committed by words alone. Dismissing the appeal, the Court of Appeal held that both these arguments were wrong. This case was decided before the House of Lords decision in *Ireland, Burstow* (below) but is entirely consistent with it. It seems clear that a telephone call can amount to an assault where it causes the victim to apprehend personal violence in the immediate future.

(Note: The **Protection from Harassment Act 1997** (as amended) contains a number of offences relating to harassment and stalking (see below) which would now likely be charged in cases involving similar circumstances.)

AROBIEKE (1987)

D had been following his victim and was looking at a train which he thought his victim might have boarded. His victim was not on the train but panicked when he saw D and tried to escape across a railway line.

The line was live and the victim was electrocuted. The court held that D was not guilty of unlawful act manslaughter because his actions did not constitute an assault. There was no apprehension by the victim of the immediate infliction of violence.

Mens rea of assault

The defendant has the mens rea of assault if he intends the victim to apprehend the immediate infliction of personal violence or is reckless as to whether the victim might do so. The mens rea of assault is subjective. It is satisfied by proof of intention or of *Cunningham* recklessness: see Ch.2. The subjective nature of the test for mens rea in assault was confirmed by the House of Lords in *Savage, Parmenter* (1991): see below.

Summary

ACTUS REUS
D must do the following:
- Cause V to fear the application of immediate, unlawful force.

MENS REA
*D must possess **one** of the following:*
- Intention to cause V to fear the application of immediate, unlawful force; or
- Subjective (*Cunningham*) recklessness as to causing V to fear the application of immediate, unlawful force.

BATTERY

Actus reus of battery

The actus reus of battery is the slightest "direct" application of force to another person thus the merest touching will suffice: *Collins v Wilcock* (1984). It is sufficiently direct if done via a medium controlled by D, e.g. D sets his dog on V or throws a brick which hits V. When D punched a mother causing her to drop her child who hit his head on the floor, this was a battery upon the child (as well as upon the mother): *Haystead v DPP* (2000). A battery has been said to require a hostile act, but in the House of Lords in *Re F* (1990) Lord Goff said:

"I respectfully doubt whether that is correct. A prank that gets out of hand; an over-friendly slap on the back; surgical treatment by a surgeon who mistakenly thinks that the patient has consented to it all these things may transcend the bounds of lawfulness, without being characterised as hostile. Indeed the suggested qualification is difficult to reconcile with the principle that any touching of another's body is, in the absence of lawful excuse, capable of amounting to a battery and a trespass."

In *Brown* (1993) it was decided that if the defendant's actions are unlawful then they also satisfy the requirement for hostility.

The actus reus of a battery can be a continuing act.

KEY CASE

FAGAN V METROPOLITAN POLICE COMMISSIONER (1969)
D had driven his car on to a policeman's foot by mistake but was slow to remove it when he realised what he had done. The court held that the actus reus of the battery was the remaining on the foot and the intention later formed to remain on the policeman's foot was sufficient mens rea.

Mens rea of battery

To have the mens rea of battery, the defendant must intend to apply force to another or be reckless as to whether such force would be applied (see for example *Venna* (1975)). The mens rea of battery is therefore satisfied by proof of intention or of *Cunningham* (subjective) recklessness, the latter requiring proof that D foresaw a risk that force would be applied but carried on with his actions regardless.

Summary

ACTUS REUS
D must do the following:
- Apply unlawful force to V.

MENS REA
*D must possess **one** of the following:*
- Intention to apply unlawful force to V; or
- Subjective (*Cunningham*) recklessness as to applying unlawful force to V.

OFFENCES AGAINST THE PERSON ACT 1861

Section 47

> **LEGISLATION HIGHLIGHTER**
>
> Section 47 of the **Offences Against the Person Act 1861.**
>
> This section makes it an offence, punishable with a maximum of five years' imprisonment, to commit "an assault occasioning actual bodily harm". The word "assault" here is used to mean either an assault or a battery. Thus for the s.47 offence there has to be actual bodily harm which is caused by either an assault or a battery.

For the s.47 offence, the following two elements are required:
  (i)   Either (a) the actus reus plus the mens rea of assault or (b) the actus reus plus the mens rea of battery.
  (ii) Actual bodily harm caused by the assault or battery.

Actus reus of s.47

> **CHECKPOINT**
>
> The term "occasion" simply means "cause" (*Roberts* (1971)).

The actus reus for the crime is both (a) the actus reus of assault or of battery, and (b) the causing of actual bodily harm by that assault or battery.

> **CHECKPOINT**
>
> Actual bodily harm was defined in the case of *Miller* (1954) as "any hurt or injury calculated to interfere with the health and comfort of the victim".

The actus reus requires there to be a causal link between the assault (or battery) and the actual bodily harm, the test of causation being an objective one of whether the actual bodily harm was a foreseeable consequence of the defendant's action. Thus, an action of the victim which is so daft or so unexpected that no reasonable person could be expected to foresee it, would break the chain of causation: see *Roberts* (above). Actual bodily harm includes any personal injury whether or not it is serious. A cut or bruise could qualify as actual bodily harm. Cutting off a substantial part of someone's hair can amount to actual bodily harm (though consent would be a defence): *DPP v Smith* (2006). Also included is psychiatric injury, although mere emotions such as fear, distress, panic or psychological symptoms which do not amount to a recognised psychiatric illness will not suffice.

KEY CASE

CHAN FOOK (1994)

D acted aggressively towards his victim and locked him in an upstairs room. The victim's evidence was that he felt abused, humiliated and frightened. D was convicted of an assault occasioning actual bodily harm. The Court of Appeal held that actual bodily harm could include psychiatric injury, though not mere emotions such as fear, distress and panic. The only evidence of psychiatric harm in this case, however, had been that of the victim and D's conviction was quashed because where psychiatric injury is alleged as the actual bodily harm, expert evidence must always be called. Otherwise, the issue should be withdrawn from the jury. This case has since been approved by the House of Lords in *Ireland, Burstow* (below).

Mens rea of s.47

The mens rea required is the mens rea for the assault or battery. No mens rea is required as to the causing of actual bodily harm see *Savage; Parmenter* (below). Thus there is no need to prove that the defendant intended or foresaw any bodily harm.

Summary

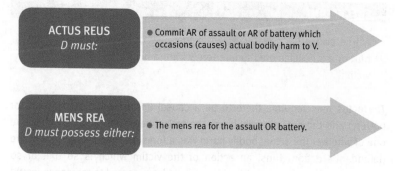

ACTUS REUS
D must:
● Commit AR of assault or AR of battery which occasions (causes) actual bodily harm to V.

MENS REA
D must possess either:
● The mens rea for the assault OR battery.

Section 20

Section 20 of the Offences Against the Person Act 1861:

"Whosoever shall unlawfully and maliciously wound or inflict any grievous bodily harm upon any other person either with or without any weapon or instrument shall be guilty of an offence ...".

Actus reus of s.20

The actus reus for s.20 is either wounding or inflicting grievous bodily harm.

CHECKPOINT

Wounding involves a complete break in the skin: *JCC v Eisenhower* (1983). A graze will be insufficient for a wound unless the skin is completely broken: *McLoughlin* (1838). Similarly, a broken collarbone is not a wound unless the skin is broken. It could, however, amount to grievous bodily harm.

Grievous bodily harm means really serious bodily harm: *DPP v Smith* (1961). There is no real difference between "really serious bodily harm" and "serious bodily harm": *Saunders* (1985).

As long it is "serious" or "really serious", psychiatric harm will satisfy the definition though where psychiatric harm is the basis of the charge, expert evidence must be called. The effect of harm on a particular individual, for example due to the age or health of the victim, should be taken into account when determining whether the harm amounts to GBH: *Bollom* (2003).

KEY CASE

IRELAND, BURSTOW (1997)

The appeals in two different cases were heard together by the House of Lords. In *Ireland*, D had made a lot of unwanted telephone calls to three women, sometimes repeated calls over a short period. When the women answered there was silence. According to expert evidence the effect of the calls in each case was that the women suffered significant psychological symptoms including palpitations, cold sweats, anxiety, insomnia, dizziness and stress. D was convicted on three counts of an assault occasioning actual bodily harm and appealed, eventually, to the House of Lords. In *Burstow*, D refused to accept that a woman wished to end the relationship he had had with her. Over a six-year period he followed her to work, repeatedly visited her house, turned up unexpectedly at places where she happened to be. He sent her hate mail, stole clothing from her washing line and scattered condoms in her garden. As a result she suffered endogenous depression with marked features of anxiety. He was convicted of maliciously inflicting grievous bodily harm contrary to s.20 and appealed, eventually, to the House of Lords. Both appeals were dismissed. It was held:

(i) that bodily harm in ss.47 and 20 included a recognisable psychiatric illness (approving *Chan Fook*, above);

(ii) the word "inflict" in s.20 was capable of embracing someone inflicting psychiatric injury upon another. One can inflict grievous bodily harm under s.20 without any physical violence being applied to the victim's body, either directly or indirectly;

(iii) making silent telephone calls causing psychiatric injury, whilst not capable of amounting to a battery, was capable of amounting to an assault and therefore could form the basis of a charge under s.47.

In *Ireland, Burstow*, the House of Lords made it clear that serious bodily harm can be "inflicted" (caused) with or without there being any physical assault and that it can be "inflicted" without there being even any personal violence at all, whether direct or indirect. Statements to the contrary in earlier cases are no longer good law. See also *Dica*, below.

Mens rea of s.20

The mens rea for s.20 is denoted by the word "maliciously". This indicates that the mens rea is satisfied by proof of either intention or *Cunningham* recklessness as to causing *some* harm. It is not necessary, however, for the defendant to intend or foresee bodily harm of the seriousness required for the actus reus of this offence. Whereas the actus reus requires the defendant to wound or to inflict "serious" bodily harm, the mens rea is established by proof that the defendant intended or foresaw some bodily harm: *Mowatt* (1968). The test is a subjective one requiring proof that the defendant intended or foresaw bodily harm, albeit not necessarily serious bodily harm: *Grimshaw* (1984).

SAVAGE; PARMENTER (1991)

Appeals in two separate cases were heard together in the House of Lords. In *Savage*, D threw a glass of beer at her victim. In the process D lost a grip of the glass itself which broke and cut the victim's wrist. D was convicted of inflicting grievous bodily harm contrary to s.20. On appeal to the Court of Appeal this was reduced to a conviction for an assault occasioning actual bodily harm contrary to s.47. D appealed to the House of Lords against this conviction, arguing that she had not foreseen that her action might cause any bodily harm. In *Parmenter*, D had caused damage to the bone structure of his baby son. At his trial on a charge that D had maliciously inflicted grievous bodily harm, contrary to s.20, the judge directed the jury that he was guilty if he *should* have foreseen some bodily harm, even if only of a minor nature. The Court of Appeal quashed the resulting conviction because the jury should have been directed not to convict unless sure that D had actually foreseen some bodily harm. The Court of Appeal refused, however, to substitute a conviction for an assault occasioning actual bodily harm contrary to s.47. The prosecution appealed against that refusal. The House of Lords dismissed D's appeal in *Savage* and allowed the prosecution's appeal in *Parmenter*. Their Lordships held: (i) there is a subjective test for the mens rea for the offence in s.20 which requires proof that the defendant foresaw the risk of causing some bodily harm; and (ii) the mens rea required for an assault occasioning actual bodily harm contrary to s.47 is the same as that for common assault, (i.e. for an assault or a battery) and for s.47 the prosecution does not have to prove that the defendant intended or foresaw any bodily harm.

Summary

ACTUS REUS D must:	• Inflict (cause) a wound or grievous bodily harm.

MENS REA D must possess **either**:	• The intention to cause some harm; or • Subjective (*Cunningham*) recklessness as to causing some harm.

LEGISLATION HIGHLIGHTER

Section 18 of the Offences Against the Person Act 1861

"Whosoever shall unlawfully and maliciously by any means whatsoever wound or cause any grievous bodily harm to any person, with intent to do some grievous bodily harm to any person, or with intent to resist or prevent the lawful apprehension or detainer of any person, shall be guilty of an offence ...".

Actus reus of section 18

The actus reus requires a "wound" or the causing of "grievous bodily harm". These expressions have the same meaning as in s.20. Under s.18 the defendant must have *caused* grievous bodily harm as opposed to *inflicted* it. However, after the decision of the House of Lords in *Ireland, Burstow* (above), there seems little, if any, difference between *causing* something and *inflicting* it.

On a charge of wounding or causing grievous bodily harm with intent under s.18, an alternative verdict of guilty of maliciously inflicting grievous bodily harm contrary to s.20 is possible. This will be relevant if the jury are not satisfied that D had the necessary intent for a conviction under s.18 but are satisfied that D committed the relevant actus reus and foresaw the risk of causing at least some bodily harm.

Mens rea of section 18

The mens rea required for the offence in s.18 is an intention. One of the following forms of intention must be proved:

(i)   an intent to cause grievous bodily harm, or
(ii) an intent to resist or prevent a (lawful) arrest or detention.

The offence is thus, unlike the offences in ss.20 and 47, one of specific intent, which is relevant where the defendant is voluntarily intoxicated (see defences in Ch.6). Nothing less than intention will suffice. It should be noted that an intention to wound is not sufficient: *Taylor* (2009).

KEY CASE

BELFON (1976)

D attacked his victim with a razor causing him serious injury. He was charged with wounding with intent to cause grievous bodily harm. The judge directed the jury that he had sufficient mens rea if he foresaw that his actions would probably cause serious injury. He appealed. The

Court of Appeal held that under s.18, recklessness was not sufficient mens rea and that an intention to cause grievous bodily harm had to be proved. The court therefore quashed D's conviction under s.18 and substituted a verdict of guilty under s.20.

Turning to the alternative intention, it appears to be enough that D intended to resist an arrest which was in fact lawful, i.e. even if D believed it to be unlawful: *Lee* (2000). D would, however, have the defence of self-defence if he used no more force than was reasonably necessary to resist an arrest which, though in fact lawful, was unlawful on the facts as D mistakenly believed them to be: *Blackburn v Bowering* (1994).

Summary

ACTUS REUS D must:	• Cause a wound or grievous bodily harm.

MENS REA D must possess **either**:	• An intention to cause grievous bodily harm; or • An intention to resist or prevent a lawful arrest or detention.

HARASSMENT AND STALKING

In 1996/7 a number of cases arose which involved the modern phenomenon of stalking, i.e. persistently pursuing someone (sometimes a lover who had jilted the accused or someone who had rebuffed the accused's sexual advances). In some of these cases the accused was charged with assault, or with offences under ss.18, 20 or 47 of the **Offences Against the Person Act 1861**. Some of these eventually resulted in the definitions of the offences being judicially widened see *Constanza* (above) and *Ireland, Burstow* (above). In the meantime Parliament was legislating to make stalking a crime. The result was the **Protection from Harassment Act 1997**. It created two new offences:

Harassment
It is an offence to pursue a course of conduct which amounts to harassment of another and which the accused knows, or ought to know, amounts to

harassment (ss.1 and 2). The statute provides no definition of harassment beyond stating that it includes alarming another or causing them distress. This is a summary offence punishable with a maximum of six months' imprisonment. As few as two incidents can amount to a course of conduct, but only if there is a sufficient connection between them: *Lau v DPP* (2000). The incidents which comprise the course of conduct (e.g. repeated abusive phone calls) could occur within a period as brief as five minutes: *Kelly* (2003). A course of conduct could be classed as a single offence of harassment even though directed at more than one person, provided those persons were a close-knit definable group (e.g. man and wife) living in the same house and the conduct was clearly aimed at each one on each occasion, even though only one might have been present on any one occasion: *DPP v Dunn* (2000).

Putting the victim in fear of violence

A person whose course of conduct causes another to fear, on at least two occasions, that violence will be used against him commits an offence under s.4 if he knows or ought to know that his course of conduct will cause the other to fear violence against him on each of those two occasions. The maximum sentence is five years' imprisonment.

It is not enough that D frightened or even "seriously frightened" his victim. The offence is not committed unless the victim feared violence would be used against the victim: *Henley* (2000). A threat of violence to the victim's family or her dog could form the basis of a prosecution, provided that (a) it caused the victim to be put in fear of violence being used against the victim and (b) D knew or ought to have known that it would cause such fear. In *R (A Child) v DPP* (2001), a threat in the presence of the victim to blow out her dog's brains caused her to fear violence to herself.

Stalking offences

From November 2012 two new offences of stalking and stalking involving fear of violence or serious alarm or distress were inserted into the **Protection from Harassment Act 1997** by the Protection of Freedoms Act 2012. The offence of stalking, now contained in s.2A of the 1997 Act, is committed if a person engages in a course of conduct which would amount to harassment, the conduct also amounts to stalking and the person whose course of conduct it is knows or ought to know that the course of conduct amounts to harassment of that other person.

Acts or omissions associated with stalking include (in particular circumstances); following a person; contacting, or attempting to contact, a person by any means; publishing any statement or other material; relating or purporting to relate to a person, or purporting to originate from a person; monitoring the use by a person of the internet, email or any other form of electronic communication; loitering in any place (whether public or private); interfering with any property in the possession of a person; watching or spying on a person.

The more serious offence of stalking involving fear of violence or serious alarm or distress under s.4 of the 1997 Act is committed where a person engages in a course of conduct which amounts to stalking and either causes another to fear, on at least two occasions, that violence will be used against them, or causes that person serious alarm or distress which has a substantial adverse effect on that persons usual day-to-day activities.

DEFENCES TO NON-FATAL OFFENCES AGAINST THE PERSON

CONSENT

The non-fatal offences against the person considered in this chapter require the prosecution to prove that **unlawful** force was threatened or used by the defendant. A person may be acting lawfully, for example, if he inflicts force in self-defence or if the alleged victim consents to the use of force. Self-defence is a general defence (i.e. it is not available only to a defendant charged with a non-fatal offence against the person) and is considered further in Ch. 6. The following is an overview of the defence of consent to non-fatal offences against the person. Note that the rules governing the defence of consent to non-fatal offences are not the same as the rules governing consent in the context of sexual offences, which are explored in Ch. 8.

In the context of non-fatal offences, the general rule is that consent is a defence to assault and battery. Such consent may be express or implied: *"Generally speaking, consent is a defence to battery; and most of the physical contacts of ordinary life are not actionable because they are impliedly consented to by all who move in society and expose themselves to the risk of bodily contact." Collins v Wilcock* (1984). Thus, consent would be a defence if D merely bumped into V in a busy street. However, consent is not a defence to crimes involving the infliction of actual bodily harm, or worse, upon the victim unless the situation is one that it is in the public interest to allow.

Consent to harm

KEY CASE

BROWN (1993)
Five Ds were involved in a series of consensual sadomasochistic sexual acts in private. During these activities the Ds inflicted injuries

upon one another. They were convicted of offences under ss.47 and 20 of the **Offences Against the Person Act 1861** and appealed on the ground that the consent of the participants made their actions lawful. The House of Lords held that all assaults causing more than merely transient harm will be unlawful, even if they are consented to, unless there are good policy reasons for allowing the victim's consent to operate as a defence.

Exceptional cases where consent is a defence even though actual bodily harm is caused include: lawful sports; dangerous exhibitions; and, reasonable surgical interference: *Attorney General's Reference (No. 6 of 1980)* (1981). In *Brown*, the House of Lords confirmed that consent can also be a defence where actual bodily harm is caused by tattooing and piercing or during rough horseplay. Consent can validly be given to the risk of serious infection during consensual sexual intercourse provided the other party gives informed consent (see below).

The following are some examples of situations in which consent as a defence to harm has been successful.

KEY CASE

BARNES (2004)
During an amateur football match, D injured another player in a crushing tackle that the prosecution alleged was late, unnecessary, reckless and too high. D appealed against his conviction for an offence contrary to s.20 of the Offences Against the Person Act 1861. The Court of Appeal held that a foul, even if sufficient to justify a sending off, is not necessarily outside the scope of the consent impliedly given by those who take part in contact sports. The jury should have been directed to determine whether D's conduct was within what could be anticipated in a normal game of football or was something "quite outside" it.

KEY CASE

WILSON (1996)
D's wife asked him to tattoo his name on her body. Using a hot knife, D burnt his initials onto her buttocks. His conviction for assault occasioning actual bodily harm was quashed on appeal. The Court of Appeal held that D's conduct was no more dangerous than tattooing. Public policy did not demand that the activity should be criminal, so the defence of consent was available.

AITKEN (1992)

During celebrations, some RAF officers drank a lot of alcohol and indulged in horseplay which included setting alight the fire resistant suit of an officer who was wearing it. The officer was severely burnt. The culprits were convicted of maliciously inflicting grievous bodily harm. Their convictions were quashed on appeal. The Court of Appeal held that consent was available as a defence if the victim had consented, or if the defendants had believed (whether reasonably or not) that the victim was consenting to their activities.

Informed consent

Where D knows that he is exposing V to a risk of harm, for example because D is infected with a serious sexually transmissible disease and has unprotected sexual intercourse with V, V's consent will be invalid unless s/he is aware of the risk s/he is taking (i.e. V's consent must be an informed consent). If V knowingly takes the risk then the consent will be a valid defence to any charge that D inflicted harm upon V by infecting V with the relevant disease.

DICA (2003)

D, who knew that he was HIV positive, had unprotected consensual sexual intercourse, with two different women with each of whom he had a long-term relationship. Each of the women subsequently tested positive for HIV. D was charged with two offences of maliciously inflicting grievous bodily harm, contrary to s.20 of the Offences Against the Person Act 1861, on the basis that he had recklessly infected each of the women with HIV. The prosecution's case was that neither woman would have agreed to sexual intercourse (protected or unprotected) with him, if she had known that he was HIV positive. The Court of Appeal held: (i) recklessly infecting another person with HIV can amount to a s.20 offence as *Clarence* (1889) was no longer good law; (ii) D was not guilty of rape since each of the women had consented to sexual intercourse; (iii) given the long-term nature of the relationships, if D had concealed the truth about his HIV condition with the result that either of the women was unaware of the risk of infection, then she was not consenting to that risk and consent would be no defence to the charge under s.20; (iv) if either of the women had known about D's HIV positive condition, then consent to run that risk would be a good defence to the charge under s.20, unlike consent to the deliberate and intentional infliction of bodily harm for the purposes of sexual gratification which did not amount to a valid defence in *Donovan* (1934), *Brown* (1994), *Boyea* (1992) and *Emmett* (1999).

Invalid consent

Consent is no defence if the victim lacks the capacity to consent, or if D obtains consent by fraud. For these purposes there are two types of fraud: (i) fraud as to D's identity; or (ii) fraud as to the nature and quality of D's act(s). Fraud as to identity has been interpreted narrowly.

KEY CASE

RICHARDSON (1999)

D, a dentist who had been suspended from practice, carried out dental treatment on patients who were unaware that she was suspended. The prosecution contended that this amounted to fraud as to D's identity and the consent of her patients was thereby vitiated (i.e. negatived). D's appeal against her convictions for assault occasioning actual bodily harm was allowed. D had not deceived her patients as to her identity but merely as to her professional qualifications.

KEY CASE

TABASSUM (2000)

D persuaded several women to take part in a cancer survey he was carrying out in order to prepare a software database to sell to doctors. This involved them removing their bras and allowing D to feel their breasts. They consented to this but would not have done so if they had known D was not medically qualified. It was held that this mistake as to the "quality" of D's act negatived their consent and, consequently, D was guilty of indecent assault. [In relation to sexual offences, the Sexual Offences Act 2003 s.76 now creates a conclusive presumption that there was no consent where the defendant intentionally deceived the victim as to the *nature* or *purpose* of the act, see Ch.8.]

CORPORAL PUNISHMENT

Corporal punishment in both state schools and private schools is now, by statute, no longer permitted. Reasonable chastisement for the purpose of correction by a parent is compatible with the European Convention on Human

Rights provided the jury is directed to take into account the following five factors when deciding whether the chastisement was reasonable:

(i)   the nature and context of D's behaviour;
(ii) its duration;
(iii) the physical and mental consequences for the child;
(iv) the age and personal characteristics of the child;
(v)   the reasons D gives for the punishment. (*H* (*2001*))

The Children Act 2004 s.58 now provides that the defence of reasonable chastisement is not available to a charge under ss.18, 20 or 47 of the **Offences Against the Person Act 1861**, nor to a charge under the Children and Young Persons Act 1933 s.1 (cruelty to someone under 16). The defence remains available to a charge of assault or battery.

. . . .

PROPOSALS FOR REFORM

As a part of the Law Commission's *Eleventh Programme of Law Reform,* Law Com. No. 330, HC 1407 (19 July 2011) the Ministry of Justice invited the Law Commission to carry out a "scoping exercise" as a "first step" towards the reform of the law in this area. The Law Commission observed that:

> "The Offences Against the Person Act 1861 is widely recognised as being outdated. It uses archaic language and follows a Victorian approach of listing separate offences for individual factual scenarios, many of which are no longer necessary (for example, the offence under section 17 of impeding a person endeavouring to save himself from a shipwreck)." (Eleventh Programme of Law Reform para 2.61)

At the time of publication the Law Commission were due to begin work on the scoping paper in early 2014.

REVISION CHECKLIST

You should now know and understand:

☐   **what is meant by "common assault";**

☐   **how to identify the offences of assault and battery and the distinction between the two offences;**

☐   **the operation of sections 47, 20 and 18 of the Offences Against the Person Act 1861 including:**

i.   what constitutes actual bodily harm;

ii.   what constitutes grievous bodily harm;

iii. what constitutes a wound;

iv. the required mens rea for each of the above offences;

☐ the operation of offences created to deal with harassment and stalking;

☐ the availability of implied consent in circumstances that may otherwise constitute a common assault;

☐ the limited nature of the availability of consent to harm;

☐ the availability of a defence of reasonable chastisement to a charge of battery.

QUESTION AND ANSWER

QUESTION

In the course of a rugby match between Northtown and Southtown Mitch, the Northtown scrum half performs a "high tackle" on John, a Southtown player for which he is penalised by the referee. As a result of the tackle John sustains bruising to his chest. John, incensed by the tackle, waits until later in the game before stamping on Mitch's ankle causing it to break. Mitch did not have the ball at the time that John stamped on his ankle.

Mitch's sister Zoe, annoyed with John for injuring Mitch, runs on to the pitch and punches John in the face, cutting his cheek and causing it to bleed.

Discuss the possible criminal liability of Mitch, John and Zoe.

ADVICE AND THE ANSWER

When dealing with problem questions which raise offences against the person there will often be overlap between the offences that may be charged. Do not be surprised if you find yourself considering more than one offence for each set of circumstances raised by the scenario. For example a broken nose will almost certainly constitute actual bodily harm (more than trivial harm) however, depending on the severity may also constitute grievous bodily harm (really serious harm) particularly if you are dealing with a vulnerable victim. In such a case it is perfectly acceptable, and indeed necessary, for you to identify the possible application of both offences to the scenario. Where there is a case for the more serious offence the less serious offence can be left to the jury as an alternative.

In order to achieve a high mark there are always certain things that you must always do. Firstly you must identify the offence or offences that you wish to consider. Refer to each offence in turn explaining why the offence appears to be relevant. An easy way to identify which offences will be relevant is by looking at the seriousness of the injury caused. Where V has suffered serious injury or a wound you will need to consider ss.20 and 18, where V has sustained a minor injury which is more than trivial you will need to consider s.47 and where no injury has been caused you will need to consider assault and/or battery. Where you have narrowed your discussion down to more than one offence considering the mens rea for each offence will differentiate between them.

Next you must define the offence with reference to relevant authority. Explain the elements of each offence (actus reus and mens rea) and define any terms that are ambiguous by referring to any authority that clarifies the meaning for example, *"the result of the decision in DPP v Smith is that grievous bodily harm is now taken to mean no more and no less than 'really serious bodily harm'"*. Once you have identified and defined the relevant offence(s) you should finish by applying them to the facts of the scenario, again, with reference to any relevant authority. Don't worry if you conclude that the offence cannot be made out on the facts, as long as your arguments are logical and accurate you will be credited for explaining why the offence does not apply.

Model answer

Mitch performs a high tackle on John which is potentially a common assault, more specifically a battery. The actus reus of battery is the application of unlawful force to the victim (*Fagan v MPC*) and the merest touching will suffice (*Collins v Willcock*). The mens rea of battery requires that the defendant either intended to apply unlawful force or was reckless as to the application of unlawful force (*Venna*). The test for recklessness is a subjective one (*Cunningham*). It would appear that Mitch satisfies the elements of the offence of battery as he applies force to John and it would appear that the application of force is intentional as this was clearly a deliberate act. Whether the force used was unlawful will be examined below.

Because John has sustained bruising, Mitch's tackle would appear to further constitute the more serious offence of assault occasioning actual bodily harm contrary to s.47 of the Offences Against the Person Act (OAPA) 1861. Section 47 requires an assault (meaning a common assault) which occasions actual bodily harm. We have already established that Mitch committed a battery on John by applying force to him, with the required intent. In *Roberts* it was determined that to "occasion" simply means to "cause". It is clear on the facts that Mitch's tackle caused the bruising that John sustained. The final thing to consider is whether bruising can constitute "actual bodily harm". Actual bodily harm means "any hurt or injury calculated to interfere with the health and comfort of the victim" (*Miller*) and John's bruising would appear to satisfy this. The mens rea required for s.47 is simply the mens rea for the battery which was discussed above. It would therefore appear that Mitch satisfies all of the elements required for a charge under s.47.

Despite the fact that Mitch appears to satisfy the requirement of both battery and s.47 it is unlikely that he will be liable for either offence. This is because there is an implied level of consent to lawful sporting activities recognised by *Brown, Barnes* and so the force applied may not be unlawful. Although Mitch's tackle was outside the rules of the game it could still be expected to occur and so it is likely that John would be taken to have impliedly consented to the tackle by engaging in the game of rugby (*Barnes*)

By stamping on Mitch's leg and breaking his ankle John would appear to be liable for causing grievous bodily harm contrary to s.18 of the OAPA 1861. The actus reus requires that the defendant caused grievous bodily harm to the victim. Grievous bodily harm means no more and no less than really serious bodily harm (*DPP v Smith*). This would appear to be the case in this instance as Mitch sustained a broken ankle. The mens rea for s.18 is intention to cause grievous bodily harm. It must be proven that John intended to cause really serious bodily harm to Mitch when he stamped on his ankle. If John lacked the mens rea for s.18 then it is likely that John will be liable for the less serious offence of maliciously inflicting grievous bodily harm contrary to s.20 of the OAPA 1861 (the mens rea of s.20 is discussed below in the context of wounding). It would appear however that by stamping on John's ankle whilst John did not have the ball, Mitch intended to cause John really serious harm. Consent would not be available as a defence to John as it would appear his actions fall entirely outside of the scope of the game (*Barnes*).

Zoe may be liable for a s.47 assault occasioning actual bodily harm or alternatively wounding under s.20 of the OAPA 1861. The elements of s.47 have already been discussed above and it would seem that Zoe has committed a battery when she applies unlawful force to John by punching him in the face. It would also appear from the facts that Zoe intended to apply unlawful force to John, given the deliberate nature of her punch. The battery has caused John's injury and a cut would be sufficient to amount to actual bodily harm.

Section 20 of the OAPA 1861 requires that the defendant maliciously wounds the victim. The actus reus requires that the defendant caused a wound. A wound is defined as any break in the continuity of the whole skin (*JCC v Eisenhower*). John's face was cut and bled and so it would appear that Zoe caused a wound. The required mens rea for s.20 is that the defendant either intended to cause "some harm" (*Savage; Parmenter*) or was subjectively reckless as to whether "some harm" would be caused. On the facts of the case it is clear that Zoe intended to cause John "some harm" as she punched him in the face. Zoe could be charged under either s.47 or s.20 of the OAPA 1861 however the maximum sentence carried by both offences is the same (five years).

Sexual offences

INTRODUCTION

The **Sexual Offences Act 2003** abolished most of the earlier offences controlling sexual activity, including rape, indecent assault, sexual intercourse with girls under 13 or 16, abduction and incest. It replaced them with a range of over 50 offences, which prohibit broadly the same range of activity. The names of some former offences are no longer used, e.g. indecent assault and incest, and some former offences have no direct replacement (e.g. abduction). Significant changes were made in relation to mistake as to consent (e.g. in rape) and mistake as to age (i.e. in offences against a child under 16). This chapter will consider a number of the key offences created by the 2003 Act.

OFFENCES REQUIRING LACK OF CONSENT

Rape

LEGISLATION HIGHLIGHTER

Section 1 of the **Sexual Offences Act 2003**

A person (A) commits an offence if:
(a) he intentionally penetrates the vagina, anus or mouth of another person (B) with his penis,
(b) B does not consent to the penetration, and
(c) A does not reasonably believe that B consents.

The court does not draw a distinction in seriousness between vaginal, anal and oral rape: *Ismail* (2005). Penetration is a continuing act from entry to withdrawal: s.79(2) Sexual Offences Act 2003 and any degree of penetration is sufficient: *Park* (2008). For the significance of this in relation to consent see below. The definition of "vagina" includes the vulva: Sexual Offences Act 2003 s.79(9).

Rape is a gender specific offence which can only be committed by a man, however it is possible for woman to be liable for the offence as a secondary party: *DPP v K and C* (1997).

According to s.79(2) of the **Sexual Offences Act 2003** penetration is a continuing act from entry to withdrawal. Thus, where during intercourse, the defendant realises that B is not, or is no longer, consenting, then any subsequent continuation of intercourse will amount to the offence, even if until that point no offence had been committed. This is similar to the law prior to the **Sexual Offences Act 2003**: *Kaitamaki* (1984).

ACTUS REUS
- D must penetrate
- the mouth, anus or vagina of another person (V)
- with his penis.
- B must not consent to the penetration.

MENS REA
- The penetration must be intentional.
- D does not have a reasonable belief in V's consent.

Assault by penetration

LEGISLATION HIGHLIGHTER

Section 2 of the **Sexual Offences Act 2003**

A person (A) commits an offence if:
(a) he intentionally penetrates the vagina or anus of another person (B) with a part of his body or anything else,
(b) the penetration is sexual,
(c) B does not consent to the penetration, and
(d) A does not reasonably believe that B consents.

The offence of assault by penetration as well as sexual assault (below) require proof that the penetration (or in the case of sexual assault, the touching) is "sexual".

CHECKPOINT

According to s.78 of the Sexual Offences Act 2003 an act can be sexual in two ways. Penetration, touching, or any other activity is sexual if a reasonable person would consider that:
(a) Whatever its circumstances or any person's purpose in relation to it, it is because of its nature, sexual, or
(b) Because of its nature it may be sexual and because of its circumstances or the purposes of any person in relation to it (or both) it is sexual.

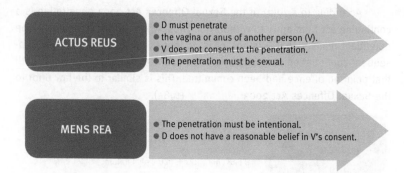

ACTUS REUS
- D must penetrate
- the vagina or anus of another person (V).
- V does not consent to the penetration.
- The penetration must be sexual.

MENS REA
- The penetration must be intentional.
- D does not have a reasonable belief in V's consent.

Sexual assault

LEGISLATION HIGHLIGHTER

Section 3 of the **Sexual Offences Act 2003**
A person (A) commits an offence if:
(a) he intentionally touches another person (B);
(b) the touching is sexual;
(c) B does not consent to the touching, and;
(d) A does not reasonably believe that B consents.

The meaning of sexual is defined above. According to s.79(8) of the **Sexual Offences Act 2003** touching includes touching:
(a) With any part of the body,
(b) With anything else,
(c) Through anything.

And in particular includes touching amounting to penetration.

A wide range of conduct has been held as being capable of amounting to sexual assault including kissing V's face: *W* (2005); touching V's breasts: *Ralston* (2005); kissing V's private parts: *Turner* (2005); and ejaculating onto V's clothes: *Bounekhla* (2006).

The offence in s.3(1) is an offence of basic intent: see *Heard* (2007), above.

| ACTUS REUS | • D must touch another person (V).
• The touching must be sexual.
• V does not consent to the touching. |

| MENS REA | • The touching must be intentional.
• D does not have a reasonable belief in V's consent. |

Section 4 of the 2003 Act makes it an offence to cause someone to engage in sexual activity without consent.

CONSENT

In these offences, a mistaken belief that B is consenting will amount to a defence only if it is a *reasonable* belief. That is different from what the law on rape previously was and the position in relation to offences outside this Act (e.g. common assault) where consent is a defence: see *Aitken* in Ch.7, above.

Whether a belief is reasonable is determined having regard to all the circumstances including any steps taken by D to ascertain whether V consents. The reasonableness of D's belief is objectively assessed. D's delusional belief that the complainant was consenting will not render his belief reasonable: *R v B* [2013].

Freedom to consent

Submission and consent are two separate things and a mere submission will not amount to consent: *Olugboja* (1981).

KEY CASE

OLUGBOJA (1981)
D threatened to keep a girl, who had already been raped earlier by another man, in his home overnight, though he made no explicit

> threats of violence and she did not resist sexual intercourse. It was held that on the evidence she had not consented but had merely submitted to intercourse under the pressure of his threat.

The principle established in *Olugboja* has been followed in cases since the 2003 Act. In *Marston* (2007) it was held to be entirely appropriate for the judge to direct the jury about the difference between compliance and consent. The courts have recognised a distinction between a reluctant (but free) agreement (which would be a valid consent) and an unwilling submission (which would not): *R v Doyle* (2010).

It is no longer the law that a woman is taken to have consented to sexual intercourse simply by virtue of being the defendant's wife: *R.* (1992).

Deception and consent

Deception by D *may* vitiate (negative) consent if the deception removes V's freedom of choice.

KEY CASE

MCNALLY [2013]

D, a female, began an internet relationship with V whilst pretending to be a boy. Later in the relationship D, presenting herself as a boy, visited V a number of times and engaged in sexual activity with her, including penetration of the V's vagina. On her final visit to V, D admitted to being female.

D pleaded guilty to six counts of assault by penetration and appealed *inter alia* asserting that, although she had deceived V as to her gender, V had consented to the act of penetration. The Court of Appeal identified that whether or not deception removed V's freedom to consent will depend on the circumstances of the particular case. Not all deceptions will vitiate consent, for example where D deceives V as to social status or wealth, however the court upheld D's convictions on the basis that D's deception as to her gender had in this case removed V's freedom to choose whether or not to have a sexual encounter with a girl.

Conditional consent

Whether or not the complainant consents to sexual penetration may depend on whether certain conditions are met. An intentional failure to meet those conditions by D may vitiate the consent otherwise given by the complainant. For example where the complainant only agrees to sexual intercourse on the basis that a condom is used and D deliberately does not wear a condom or removes the condom during intercourse this may negate the consent that was earlier given: *Assange v Sweden* [2013]. Failure to comply with the conditions must be deliberate or intentional, for example where V agrees to have sexual intercourse with D on the basis that D will not ejaculate inside of her, D will not be liable if he ejaculates prematurely or accidentally but only if he deliberately ejaculates inside his partner's vagina against her wishes: *R (F) v DPP* [2013].

Capacity to consent

The complainant must have sufficient capacity to be able to make a choice, this includes having a sufficient understanding of the sexual nature of the act so as to be able to agree to it: *R v C* [2009].

"Drunken consent"

Where a person is voluntarily intoxicated but retains the capacity (and freedom) to consent, their drunken consent will be valid even if the decision is not one which they would have made had they been sober.

KEY CASE

BREE (2007)
Clarifying the position on consent affected by voluntary intoxication Sir Igor Judge stated:

"A "drunken consent is still consent". In the context of consent to intercourse, the phrase lacks delicacy, but, properly understood, it provides a useful shorthand accurately encapsulating the legal position... If through drink (or for any other reason) [the complainant] has lost her capacity to choose... she is not consenting... However, where [the complainant] has voluntarily consumed even substantial quantities of alcohol, but nevertheless remains capable of choosing whether or not to have intercourse, and in drink agrees to do so, this would not be rape."

Presumptions about consent

Sections 75 and 76 of the 2003 Act set out evidential and conclusive presumptions respectively regarding consent. These sections apply to the four offences (in the 2003 Act) mentioned above but do not apply to offences outside the Act where consent is a defence.

Evidential (rebuttable) presumptions

According to s.75 , unless evidence is adduced to the contrary, where one of the specified circumstances in the section exists, and the accused (A) knows it exists, B is taken not to have consented and A is taken not to have reasonably believed that B consented. The specified circumstances are where:

(1) at the time of (or immediately before) the relevant act any violence was used against B (or anyone else) or B was caused to fear that it was being used or would be used, or;

(2) at the time of the relevant act:

   (a) B was asleep or unconscious;

   (b) B was (and the accused was not) unlawfully detained;

   (c) B was, due to physical disability, unable to communicate consent or lack of consent, or;

   (d) there had, without B's consent, been administered to (or caused to be taken by) B a substance capable of causing B to be stupefied or overpowered.

In order to rebut a presumption under s.75 the accused must raise some evidence "beyond the fanciful or speculative": *Ciccarelli* [2011].

Conclusive (irrebuttable) presumptions

Under s.76, it is conclusively presumed (i.e. once established the accused cannot rebut the presumption) that B did not consent and that the accused (A) did not believe that B consented if A intentionally deceived B as to the nature or purpose of the act (see for example *Williams* [1923]) or he intentionally induced B to consent by impersonating someone known personally to B (see for example *Elbekkay* [1995]).

KEY CASE

R v BINGHAM [2013]

D, using a false identity, contacted his girlfriend, V, via a social networking site. Over a period of time a relationship developed and D convinced V to send him pictures of her posing topless. Thereafter D threatened to send the images to V's employer and post them online unless V agreed to perform sexual acts over the internet. V complied with D's demands and D was charged with causing a person to engage in sexual activity without consent. The trial judge ruled that the prosecution could rely on the presumption created by s.76 of the **Sexual Offences Act 2003**, namely that, having proved that D intentionally deceved V as to the purpose of the relevant act, it could be conclusively presumed that V did not consent.

The Court of Appeal, allowing D's appeal against conviction, held that, whilst V had been deceived as to D's identity she had not been deceived as to the purpose of the act as she was aware, that at least in part, D's purpose was sexual gratification. The case should have proceeded under s.74 (above) on the question of whether D's deception removed V's freedom to consent. In any event s.76 of the **Sexual Offences Act 2003** must be strictly construed.

SEXUAL OFFENCES AGAINST UNDER-AGED PERSONS

The offences in ss.5 to 8 are exactly the same as the offences in ss.1 to 4, respectively, except that these latter offences are committed when B (the victim) is aged under 13, and B's consent is no defence.

For the offences in ss.5 to 8, there is no defence of mistaken belief as to either age or consent.

KEY CASE

G (2006)

D appealed against his conviction for rape of a girl under 13, contrary to **Sexual Offences Act 2003** s.5. He claimed that, himself a 15-year-old, he had believed her to be 15, i.e. over 13. He argued that because the offence in s.5 did not allow a defence based on such a belief, it was incompatible with art.6(2) of the **European Convention on Human Rights** (which sets out the presumption of innocence). The Court of Appeal held that there is no incompatibility with art.6 where a statute creates a strict liability offence, thus imposing liability in the absence of blameworthiness. Article 6 is concerned not with the definition of a crime but with the fairness of the criminal process.

Sections 9 and 10 create the offences of sexual activity with a child under 16 (s.9) and causing a child under 16 to engage in sexual activity (s.10). In each case:
   (i)   consent of the victim is no defence;
   (ii) if the child victim is under 16, the defendant is not guilty if he *reasonably* believed the victim to be over 16;
   (iii) there is no defence of mistaken belief as to age, if the child victim is under 13.

The requirement that the defendant's belief (that the victim is over 16) must be objectively reasonable is a change to what the law previously was: see *B. v DPP* (2000) and *K* (2001).

You should now know and understand:

☐ the elements of the offence of rape;

☐ the elements of the offences of assault by penetration and sexual assault;

☐ the meaning of "sexual" in the context of the two offences above;

☐ the definition of consent in relation to sexual offences;

☐ the distinction between submission and consent;

☐ that deception may negative consent where it removes the complainant's freedom of choice;

☐ when a complainant may lack capacity to consent;

☐ the effect of voluntary intoxication on consent;

☐ the operation of evidential presumptions in relation to consent;

☐ the position relating to consent where the alleged victim is under 16.

QUESTION AND ANSWER

QUESTION

Suzy and Beth, both aged over 18, went out for a drink to celebrate the fact that Beth had recently received a promotion in the office where they both work. Later in the evening they were joined by two of their colleagues, Chris and Darren. After a few hours in the pub Suzy decided to leave and Darren, who had not been drinking, offered to give her a lift home. Beth and Chris decided to go clubbing.

Half-way home Darren stopped the car and told Suzy that he "really fancied her" and that he knew she felt the same. He then reached across and grabbed Suzy's breast through her top. Suzy pushed his hand away and asked him to take her home but instead Darren locked the car doors and said "come on, you knew what was going to happen when you got in the car". At Darren's insistence Suzy then, reluctantly, performed oral sex on him following which Darren took her home.

After leaving the club Beth kissed Chris following which Chris asked Beth back to his flat where they engaged in sexual intercourse for which Beth requested he use a condom. Both Chris and Beth were very drunk and the next day Beth was horrified to discover that she and Chris had had sex, something she would not have done had she been sober.

Discuss the potential criminal liability of Darren and Chris.

Consent will usually be a key issue when dealing with a question involving sexual offences. It is important to be able to recognise the offences to which consent is an important element (namely rape, assault by penetration, sexual assault and the offence of causing a person to engage in sexual activity without their consent) and the offences where consent is irrelevant, for example offences involving children under 16.

Once you have identified whether consent is a key issue you must define consent. The definition of consent is found in s.74 of the **Sexual Offences Act 2003** and requires an agreement "by choice" where the person has the "freedom and capacity" to make that choice.

The issue of consent always raises two questions. Firstly whether in fact V consented or not and secondly whether the D had a "reasonable belief" in consent. When determining whether there was in fact consent you will normally need to consider the circumstances that existed at the time. For example if V was placed under pressure at the time of the relevant act you may need to consider whether V consented or merely submitted (see *Olugboja; Doyle*) or if V was voluntarily intoxicated you should consider whether V retained the capacity to consent (see *Bree*). Whether D had a reasonable belief in consent is established by considering all of the circumstances including any steps taken by D to ascertain whether V consents. D's belief must be objectively reasonable (*R v B*).

Remember in certain situations, for example where V had a substance administered to them or where they were asleep or otherwise unconscious at the time of the relevant act, s.75 of the Sexual Offences Act 2003 creates an evidential (rebuttable) presumption against consent (and against a reasonable belief in consent). This means that unless evidence is produced to the contrary it will be presumed that, if the relevant circumstances existed at the time of the relevant act, V did not consent, nor did D have a reasonable belief in consent.

Where a presumption under s.76 applies the effect is that there is a conclusive presumption against consent/reasonable belief in consent.

Answer plan:

1 Darren may be liable for a sexual assault contrary to s.3 of the **Sexual Offences Act** (SOA) 2003 when he grabs Suzy's breast. Sexual assault requires the intentional sexual touching of V, without V's consent and without D having a reasonable belief in V's consent.

2 Darren has touched Suzy, it does not matter that she is wearing clothes as touching can be "through anything" (SOA 2003 s.79(8)). The touching of Suzy's breast would appear to be "sexual" (*Ralston*) because of the circumstances and Darren's purpose in relation to it (SOA 2003 s.78).

3 Consent means agreement by choice with the freedom and capacity to make that choice (SOA 2003 s.74). Suzy slaps Darren's hand away which suggests she does not consent to the touching.

4 Whether or not Darren has a reasonable belief in consent is to be assessed having regard to all of the circumstances including any steps taken by Darren to ascertain whether Suzy consents. The reasonableness of his belief is objectively assessed. (R v B)

5 Darren may also be liable for rape contrary to s.1 of the SOA 2003. Rape requires the intentional penetration of the mouth, anus or vagina of V, without V's consent and without D having a reasonable belief in V's consent. Darren appears to have penetrated Suzy's mouth. No distinction is drawn between vaginal, anal and oral rape (*Ishmail*).

6 As above, consent means agreement by choice with the freedom and capacity to make that choice (SOA 2003 s.74). The fact that Darren has locked Suzy in the car may suggest that Suzy does not have the "freedom" to make the choice. In *Olugboja* it was held that submission does not necessarily amount to consent and it appears on the facts that Suzy may simply have submitted. The jury would have to decide whether Suzy reluctantly (but freely) agreed or whether she unwillingly submitted (*Doyle*).

7 If Suzy was unlawfully detained at the time of the relevant act then there will be an evidential presumption against consent (and against D having a reasonable belief in consent). It appears that Suzy was unlawfully detained as Darren locked the doors to the car after she requested he take her home. Darren would be required to rebut the presumption against consent by adducing evidence to show that Suzy

did in fact consent, this evidence should be more than "fanciful or speculative" (*Ciccarelli*). This would appear to be difficult on the facts. In any case, having regard to the circumstances it would appear difficult to establish a reasonable belief in consent on behalf of Darren even if the presumption were to be rebutted.

8 Chris may be liable for rape (see above) as it appears he has intentionally penetrated Beth's vagina.

9 If Beth retained the capacity (and freedom) to make a choice then any consent that she gave at the time the sexual intercourse took place will be valid despite the fact that she was (voluntarily) intoxicated and despite the fact she would not normally have engaged in sexual intercourse had she been sober. Essentially her drunken consent is still a valid consent (*Bree*). Evidence that Beth requested Chris use a condom may establish that she retained the capacity to consent and did, in fact, consent to the activity. Beth's consent may be conditional on Chris having used a condom (*Assange*).

10 The reasonableness of Chris's belief must be established by looking at the circumstances including any steps he has taken to ascertain if Beth consented. Evidence that Beth kissed him and requested he use a condom may help to establish the reasonableness of Chris's belief.

Homicide

INTRODUCTION

Homicides are unlawful killings. The major categories are murder and manslaughter which itself can be broken down into a number of types. Voluntary manslaughter involves killings that otherwise would be treat as murder but where the defendant has one of three special partial defences available to him. Involuntary manslaughter (killing without the required intent for murder) includes constructive manslaughter, gross negligence manslaughter and reckless manslaughter. Other unlawful killings include corporate manslaughter, causing death whilst driving and causing or allowing the death of a child or vulnerable adult.

MURDER

> **CHECKPOINT**
>
> Murder, a common law offence, is the unlawful killing of a human being under the Queen's peace with malice aforethought.

Actus reus

The killing must be of a human being. The unlawful killing of an unborn child therefore is not murder and is covered by other offences. On the other hand, if injuries are inflicted on an unborn child which is then born alive and subsequently dies of the pre-natal injuries, that can amount to murder (subject to the formation of the necessary mens rea) or constructive manslaughter (see below): *Attorney General's Reference (No. 3 of 1994)*.

"Under the Queen's peace" means that the killing of an enemy in the course of war will not be murder. It should be noted however that this is quite limited in scope. A soldier who kills otherwise than in the course of battle, for example by killing a prisoner under his control, may be liable for murder.

The killing must be unlawful. Certain defences (see Ch.6), for example self-defence, can make a killing lawful.

It is also necessary for there to have been a death. Death is established upon the irreversible death of the brain stem: *Malcherek, Steel* (1981). The requirement that the death must occur within a year and a day of the defendant's action was abolished by the Law Reform (Year and Day Rule) Act 1996. However, no proceedings may be commenced without the consent of the Attorney General if either the injury which is alleged to have caused the death occurred more than three years before the death or the defendant has previously been convicted of an offence alleged to be connected with the death.

It is, of course, necessary for the prosecution to establish that the defendant caused the death. For cases on causation see Ch.1.

Mens rea

The mens rea for murder has traditionally been described as "malice aforethought". This expression is now inappropriate and has been described as "doubly misleading" (*Attorney General's Reference (No.3 of 1994)*). The accused does not have to have acted maliciously, i.e. out of malice. Nor does the accused have to have premeditated the killing.

CHECKPOINT

The mens rea of murder (malice aforethought) is established by proof that the accused had, at the time he carried out the act which caused the death, either (i) an intention to kill or (ii) an intention to cause grievous bodily harm: *Moloney* (1985).

Before 1957, there was a third alternative which was termed constructive malice. Thus it used to be sufficient for the prosecution to establish that the killing occurred whilst the defendant was committing a crime of violence: *DPP v Beard* (1920). Constructive malice was abolished by the Homicide Act 1957.

The possibility remains that someone can be convicted of murder despite having no intention to kill and despite not even foreseeing that death might occur provided that he intended grievous bodily harm. Over the years there has been criticism of this. It has been suggested that the mens rea required for murder should be limited to an intention to kill, (see for example the minority speeches in the House of Lords in *Cunningham* (1981)). It is now, however, generally accepted that abolition of the alternative strand (an intention to cause grievous bodily harm) is a matter for the legislature. Until the legislature changes the law, the two strands of mens rea remain and thus an intention to cause grievous bodily harm is sufficient mens rea for murder. [For the Law Commission's proposed reforms, see below.]

Foresight of consequence

At one stage it seemed that a person was deemed to have the intention to kill or to cause grievous bodily harm if that was a natural consequence of his actions. This is very definitely not now the case. Intention is a subjective matter. Section 8 of the **Criminal Justice Act 1967** provides that a person is not to be taken as intending the consequences of his act simply because that consequence was natural and probable, but a jury must consider all the evidence before deciding whether they are satisfied that he had the necessary intention. For the current law on the meaning of "intention", see *Moloney, Hancock and Shankland, Nedrick* and especially *Woollin*, all set out in Ch.2.

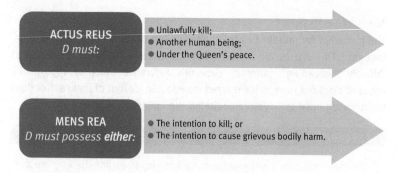

ACTUS REUS
D must:
- Unlawfully kill;
- Another human being;
- Under the Queen's peace.

MENS REA
*D must possess **either**:*
- The intention to kill; or
- The intention to cause grievous bodily harm.

VOLUNTARY MANSLAUGHTER

There are two main kinds of manslaughter: voluntary and involuntary manslaughter. Voluntary manslaughter covers the situation where the defendant has the necessary actus reus and mens rea for murder but is able to rely on one of three particular defences. Those three defences are:

(i) loss of control,

(ii) diminished responsibility, and

(iii) killing in the course of a suicide pact.

These defences are only defences to murder. If any one of these defences is successful, it does not result in an acquittal. It merely reduces what would be a murder conviction to manslaughter. The practical difference this achieves is that the accused is still convicted of a crime, manslaughter, but it does not quite carry the public stigma of a murder conviction and the judge has a discretion as to what sentence to impose. A murder conviction leaves the judge no option but to pass a life sentence whereas a manslaughter conviction allows the judge to pass any sentence up to life imprisonment. On the other hand, in the case of any other crime, the judge can take any mitigating factor, such as loss of control, into account when sentencing.

Loss of control

The Coroners and Justice Act 2009 (C&JA) (which came into force on the 4th of October 2010) abolished the defence of provocation (previously found in s.3 of the **Homicide Act 1957**) and replaced it with a new defence of "loss of control" (ss.54–55 of the C&JA 2009). The loss of control defence is expressly narrower in scope than the old defence of provocation, with parliament intending to rule out the use of the defence in certain situations. This will be discussed below. The Court of Appeal have subsequently described the loss of control defence as having "raised the bar": *Clinton* [2012] and as being "much more limited": *Dawes* [2013] than the previous defence of provocation.

LEGISLATION HIGHLIGHTER

Section 54 Coroners and Justice Act 2009

(1) Where a person ("D") kills or is a party to the killing of another ("V"), D is not to be convicted of murder if—

    (a) D's acts and omissions in doing or being a party to the killing resulted from D's loss of self-control,

    (b) the loss of self-control had a qualifying trigger, and

    (c) a person of D's sex and age, with a normal degree of tolerance and self-restraint and in the circumstances of D, might have reacted in the same or in a similar way to D.

D's acts and omissions in doing or being party to the killing resulted from D's loss of self control (s.54(1)(a))

The first element required to establish the defence is that there is evidence of a loss of self control, although s.54(2) provides that it is not necessary that the loss of self control is sudden. In *Clinton* the Court of Appeal identified that "in reality, the greater the level of deliberation, the less likely that it will be that the killing followed a true loss of self control" however in *Dawes* the court acknowledged that "different individuals in different situations do not react identically, nor respond immediately" and that therefore a delayed reaction to "circumstances of extreme gravity" may still give rise to the defence. The Explanatory Notes to the 2009 Act provide some further clarification:

> "Although subsection (2) in the new partial defence makes clear that it is not a requirement for the new partial defence that the

loss of self control be sudden, it will remain open, as at present, for the judge (in deciding whether to leave the defence to the jury) and the jury (in determining whether the killing did in fact result from a loss of self-control and whether the other aspects of the partial defence are satisfied) to take into account any delay between a relevant incident and the killing."

KEY CASE

R v CLINTON [2012]

In this case the Court of Appeal underlined the basic principles of the new defence. The entire loss of control defence is contained in sections 54 and 55 of the Coroners and Justice Act 2009. The previous defence of provocation no longer exists (s.56). In order for the defence of loss of control to be available to D there must be some evidence of a loss of control by D. Whether the evidence of D's loss of control is sufficient is a question of law to be determined by the judge. In order for the defence to be successfully pleaded all elements of the defence must be present. If there is evidence capable of supporting all elements of the defence then it is for the prosecution to disprove the defence beyond all reasonable doubt.

Evidence of a loss of self control will have been raised if a judge would consider that a properly directed jury would be able to conclude that the defence might apply. If this is the case, the jury must assume that the defence is satisfied unless the prosecution prove beyond reasonable doubt that it is not: s.54(5) and (6).

The loss of self control had a qualifying trigger (s.54(1)(b))

The defence requires the loss of control to have been caused by a "qualifying trigger". S.55 of the 2009 Act creates two potential triggers. A loss of control can be said to have been caused by a qualifying trigger if it was:

- Attributable to D's fear of SERIOUS VIOLENCE from V against D or another identified person (s.55(3)); OR
- Attributable to thing(s) said or done or both which (a) constituted circumstances of an extremely grave character AND (b) caused D to have a justifiable sense of being seriously wronged (s.55(4)). Note this is not where D incited the thing said or done in order to provide an excuse for violence (s.55(6)); OR
- Attributable to a combination of both of the above (s.55(5))

Trigger one—Fear of serious violence

For this qualifying trigger to apply D must fear serious violence from the victim either against themselves or another identified person. There appear to be two situations in which this trigger will apply. The first is where D cannot plead self defence because, although they fear violence from V there is no imminent threat of attack. The second is where D cannot plead self defence because the amount of force used is excessive.

KEY CASE

WARD [2012]

D, D's brother and the deceased (V) were friends. After a day of drinking D's brother and V began an argument which turned violent. V, who had a reputation for violence attacked and head-butted D's brother. D went to the aid of his brother, striking V with a pick axe handle a number of times, killing him. D was charged with murder and pleaded guilty to manslaughter due to a loss of self control based on his fear of serious violence from V towards his brother.

Trigger two—Attributable to things said or done or both which constituted circumstances of an extremely grave character AND caused D to have a justifiable sense of being seriously wronged.

For this qualifying trigger to apply, three things must be established. Firstly, something must be said or done (or a combination of both) to D which caused D to lose self control. Secondly, the thing said or done (or both) must have constituted "circumstances of an extremely grave character" and finally D must have had a "justifiable sense of being seriously wronged". The act is silent on whether the test for trigger two is subjective or objective but the Court of Appeal in *Clinton* established that both elements of the test are objectively assessed.

KEY CASE

DPP v CAMPLIN (1978)

D, a 15-year-old boy, hit a 50-year-old man over the head and killed him. D's defence was provocation. He claimed the deceased had forcibly buggered him and then had laughed at him whereupon D lost his self control and fatally attacked the deceased. The judge directed the jury (as to whether the alleged provocation was enough to make a reasonable man act as D had done) to consider the effect the alleged provocation would have had on an adult man. The House of Lords reduced D's murder conviction to manslaughter. Their Lordships held that the judge

ought to have directed the jury to consider the effect the alleged provocation would have had on a person of the same sex and age as D, i.e.
would it have been enough to make a reasonable 15-year-old boy react
as D had done? It was held that the "reasonable man" means a person
having the power of self control of an ordinary person of the sex and
age of the accused and in other respects sharing such of the accused's
characteristics as would affect the gravity of the provocation.

It is submitted that the facts of a case like *Camplin* would now fit squarely
within trigger two of the loss of control defence. D was raped (something
done) and then taunted by the man who raped him (something said), both
the rape and the taunt about being the victim of a rape would appear to
constitute "circumstances of an extremely grave character" and it appears
reasonable to conclude that in the circumstances D would have a "justifiable" sense of being seriously wronged.

An example of a case that would not appear to satisfy trigger two is the
case of *Doughty* (1986) where the Court of Appeal substituted a manslaughter conviction for the defendant's original conviction for murder on the
basis that there had been evidence of "things done" which may have constituted provocation. In that case, the defendant killed his infant son as a
result of his persistent crying. It appears to have been Parliament's express
intention to remove cases such as *Doughty* from the scope of the defence.
This is supported by the decision of the Court of Appeal in *Zebedee* [2012]. D
killed his father who was suffering from a severe form of senile dementia and
who soiled himself twice in a short space of time. The court held that whilst
there was clearly evidence of something done by the victim to D it did not
constitute "circumstances of an extremely grave character" nor was it capable of providing D a "justifiable" sense of being seriously wronged.

Section 55(6) of the **Coroners and Justice Act 2009** prevents the triggers
from being used where D incited the thing said or done as an excuse to use
violence. In *Dawes* the Court of Appeal held that merely behaving badly or
"looking for trouble" does not exclude the application of a qualifying trigger
unless the actions were intended to provide D with the "excuse or opportunity to use violence". Similarly where the thing said or done constitutes
"sexual infidelity" it must be disregarded and cannot be used as the basis for
a qualifying trigger however in *Clinton* [2012] the Court of Appeal determined
that whilst sexual infidelity cannot not form the basis of a qualifying trigger, if
an admissible trigger is present sexual infidelity may be considered as part of
the "context" in which that trigger may arise. It should also be noted that the
loss of self control defence does not apply where D acts in considered desire
for revenge: s.54(4).

(Note: the approach taken in this case is virtually identical to the "normal person" test which forms a part of the loss of self control defence (see below)).

The "normal person" test (s.54(1)(c))

If D has lost self control and a qualifying trigger is satisfied, the final element of the loss of self control defence is a normal person test.

CHECKPOINT

The test will be satisfied if a "person of D's age and sex, with a normal degree of tolerance and self restraint and in the circumstances of D, might have reacted in the same or in a similar way to D."

The circumstances of D are "all of D's circumstances other than those whose only relevance to D's conduct is that they bear on D's general capacity for tolerance and self restraint": s.54(3). The fact that D is voluntarily intoxicated at the relevant time is not a "circumstance" for the purposes of the reasonable person test: *Asmelash* [2013]. It should be noted that whilst sexual infidelity is excluded from forming the basis of a qualifying trigger it is not excluded in the context of the reasonable person test and may arguably therefore constitute a "circumstance".

Diminished responsibility

Section 52 of the **Coroners and Justice Act 2009** made significant amendments to the defence of diminished responsibility although the defence is still found in **Homicide Act 1957** s.2. If a defendant can prove on a balance of probabilities a defence of diminished responsibility, he will be guilty of manslaughter rather than murder.

LEGISLATION HIGHLIGHTER

Section 2 of the **Homicide Act 1957** (as amended)

(1) A person ("D") who kills or is a party to the killing of another is not to be convicted of murder if D was suffering from an abnormality of mental functioning which—
   (a) arose from a recognised medical condition;
   (b) substantially impaired D's ability to do one or more of the things mentioned in subsection (1A); and
   (c) provides an explanation for D's acts and omissions in doing or being a party to the killing.

(1A) Those things are—

(a) to understand the nature of D's conduct;
(b) to form a rational judgment;
(c) to exercise self-control.

Abnormality of mental functioning

The requirement of an abnormality of mental functioning replaced the previous requirement that D must suffer from an abnormality of mind. The term abnormality of mental functioning was introduced to make it easier for medical experts as the term abnormality of mind has no basis in psychiatry.

KEY CASE

BYRNE (1960)

D had strangled his victim and then mutilated her body. He claimed he was subject to an irresistible or almost irresistible impulse because of perverted sexual desires which overcame him and had done so since he was a boy. The Court of Appeal quashed his conviction for murder because the trial judge had misdirected the jury that s.2 of the 1957 Act was irrelevant here. The court said that the defence covered the mind's activities in all its aspects and the ability to control one's physical acts.

In *Byrne* (1960), Lord Parker C.J. defined an abnormality of mind as being "a state of mind so different from that of ordinary human beings the reasonable man would term it abnormal". It is uncertain whether the courts will apply a similarly wide definition to the term abnormality of mental functioning.

Arising from a recognised medical condition

There is no statutory definition of this term but the courts have accepted adjustment disorder: *Brown* [2011], post-traumatic stress disorder (PTSD): *Janiszewski* [2012] and Asperger's Syndrome: *Spencer* [2013] as medical conditions capable of forming the basis of a diminished responsibility plea. The Court of Appeal in *Dowds* [2012] appears to endorse its earlier decisions in *Wood* [2008] and *Stewart* [2009] that alcoholism or alcohol dependency syndrome will be capable of giving rise to the defence. Some further examples of conditions recognised under the old formulation of the diminished responsibility defence are: depression: *Seers* (1984); epilepsy: *Campbell* (1997); psycopathy: *Byrne* (1960); schizophrenia: *Erskine* (2009).

It is submitted that these conditions would likely be accepted under the new formulation of the defence.

Substantially impairs D's ability

D's abnormality of mental functioning must substantially impair his ability to do one of three things, namely:

(a) understand the nature of his conduct;

(b) form a rational judgement; or

(c) exercise self control.

In *Lloyd* (1967), "substantially" was held to mean less than total but more than trivial. In *Brown* [2011] it was held that "substantially impaired" does not carry a different meaning to "substantial impairment".

Provides an explanation for D being a party to the killing

According to s.2(1B) of the **Coroners and Justice Act 2009** D's abnormality of mental functioning will provide an explanation where the abnormality causes or is a significant contributory factor in causing D to carry out that conduct.

Intoxication and diminished responsibility

The general position is that where the accused pleads diminished responsibility but was also intoxicated at the time of the killing, the jury should discount the intoxication. The intoxication itself will not amount to an abnormality of mental functioning: *Dowds*.

KEY CASE

R v Dowds [2012]

D was convicted of the murder of his partner having stabbed her around 60 times in the neck and chest whilst voluntarily intoxicated. At his trial D sought, *inter alia*, to rely upon the defence of diminished responsibility arguing that his acute intoxication amounted to a recognised medical condition. The trial judge ruled that voluntary acute intoxication was not capable of forming the basis of a diminished responsibility plea. D was convicted of murder and appealed on the basis that the judge was incorrect to refuse to allow him to raise diminished responsibility before the jury.

The Court of Appeal held that, even though acute intoxication is recognised by the World Health Organisation as a medical condition, the presence of a "recognised medical condition" is a "necessary, but not always sufficient condition to raise the issue of diminished responsibility". Voluntary acute intoxication is not capable of forming the basis of a diminished responsibility plea and the defendant's murder conviction was upheld.

Diminished responsibility and insanity: relationship and burdens of proof

Insanity is a general defence to all crimes (except possibly those of strict liability, see Ch.6). If the defence of insanity succeeds, it results in a special verdict, "Not guilty by reason of insanity". Diminished responsibility is a defence only to murder and if successful reduces what would be a murder conviction to a conviction for manslaughter. Thus, on a murder charge, either defence can be advanced. Diminished responsibility as a concept is wider than insanity. If both defences are advanced and insanity is proved, then the correct verdict is an insanity verdict. Where the accused pleads diminished responsibility or insanity the burden of proof rests upon the accused to establish the defence on a balance of probabilities. It could occur, however, that the accused pleads diminished responsibility and it is the prosecution who argues that insanity is the proper verdict. In that case, the prosecution has the burden of proving insanity beyond all reasonable doubt. If the prosecution fails to do that, then the court will have to decide whether the accused has established that it is more likely than not that he was affected by diminished responsibility.

KEY CASE

LAMBERT, ALI AND JORDAN (2000)
Article 6.2 of the **European Convention on Human Rights** sets out the presumption of innocence. Section 2(2) of the **Homicide Act 1957** places upon the defendant the burden of proving diminished responsibility. The Court of Appeal held that s.2(2) does not violate art.6.2 of the Convention, because s.2(2) relates to a "special defence or exception" intended for the benefit of defendants and Parliament has specifically placed the burden of proof on the defendant.

The reverse burden of proof in the context of the reformulated diminished responsibility defence has been described as "deliberate and entirely comprehensible": *Foye* [2013]

Suicide pacts

LEGISLATION HIGHLIGHTER

Section 4(1) of the **Homicide Act 1957**:

"It shall be manslaughter and shall not be murder for a person acting in pursuance of a suicide pact between him and another

> to kill the other or be a party to the other being killed by a third person."

The burden of proof rests on the accused to establish the defence on a balance of probabilities: s.4(2). This reverse legal burden of proof is compatible with the European Convention on Human Rights: *Attorney General's Reference (No.1 of 2004)*.

Note that the Suicide Act 1961 abolished the crime of suicide and, with it, the crime of attempted suicide. By virtue of that same 1961 Act, however, it is still an offence to encourage or assist suicide, confirmed by the House of Lords in *The Queen on the application of Dianne Pretty v DPP* (2001). The Court of Appeal recently revisited the issue of assisted suicide in *Nicklinson v the Ministry of Justice* [2013] confirming that neither the common law defence of necessity nor Article 8 of the European Convention on Human Rights can provide an exception to the offence of encouraging or assisting suicide. If the law in this area is to change it would be the responsibility of the legislature to do so.

Section 4 of the **Homicide Act 1957**, however, deals with the situation where the accused is charged, not with attempting his own suicide (now no longer criminal) nor with aiding or abetting another suicide, but with murder. This could, for example, occur where the accused and another agree that they both intend to die and pursuant to that agreement, they lock themselves in a room, each take sleeping pills and the accused turns on the gas tap. A rescuer breaks down the door by which time the accused has not, but his partner has, succumbed to the lack of oxygen and died of asphyxiation.

INVOLUNTARY MANSLAUGHTER

Involuntary manslaughter is the term given to an unlawful homicide where the necessary mens rea for murder is not present. There are two main kinds of involuntary manslaughter: unlawful act manslaughter, and manslaughter by gross negligence. A third, smaller, branch sometimes referred to as "reckless manslaughter" is also considered briefly below.

Constructive (or unlawful act) manslaughter
In order to establish liability for constructive manslaughter D must have committed an unlawful act, the unlawful act must be dangerous, the unlawful act must have caused death, and D must have intended the unlawful act.

Unlawful act

To be an unlawful act for the purpose of constructive manslaughter, the act must amount to a crime. However, not all crimes are unlawful acts for this purpose. Thus a lawful act which becomes unlawful only as a result of negligence or carelessness, e.g. (driving) does not amount to an unlawful act: *Andrews v DPP* (1937). Even in the case of a crime which does not fall within the latter category, (e.g. assault), there is no unlawful act unless the *crime* is committed. Thus, it is not an unlawful act to commit the actus reus of the crime unless the mens rea is also present. Nor is it an unlawful act if the accused has a defence such as consent or self-defence.

KEY CASE

ANDREWS V DPP (1937)

D had been driving dangerously and knocked over and killed a pedestrian. He was convicted of manslaughter. The House of Lords held that careless driving was a lawful act done with a degree of carelessness sufficient to make it a statutory offence. It was not an unlawful act for the purposes of manslaughter. It followed that for a manslaughter conviction, the prosecution had to establish gross negligence. (For the lesser offences of causing death by dangerous driving and causing death by careless driving, see below.)

KEY CASE

LAMB (1967)

D and his friend were playing with a revolver. Knowing that there were bullets in two of the chambers and also that neither bullet was in the chamber opposite the barrel, D believed that the gun would not fire. He failed to realise that, on the trigger being pulled, the cylinder of chambers would automatically rotate. He aimed it and fired it at point blank range at his friend, who was killed. He was charged with manslaughter. The judge directed the jury that the accused had committed an unlawful act even if he had not intended to alarm or to injure. He was convicted. Allowing his appeal, the Court of Appeal held that there was no unlawful assault without the mens rea for assault. Although D might have been guilty on the basis of gross negligence, the judge had misdirected the jury as to what amounted to an unlawful act. The conviction was quashed.

When will the unlawful act be "dangerous"?

For a conviction of constructive manslaughter, the unlawful act must have been dangerous.

In *Church* (1966) it was decided that the test for dangerousness was whether "all sober and reasonable people would inevitably recognise must subject the other person to, at least, the risk of some harm resulting therefrom, albeit not serious harm". By harm, is meant, physical harm. Shock, distress or emotion will not suffice.

KEY CASE

R v JM and SM [2012]

V, a nightclub bouncer, and JM and SM were involved in a violent affray outside of the nightclub where V was employed. JM was the instigator of the affray and both JM and SM were involved in it. Although it was not established whether JM and SM had directed any violence towards V it was accepted that V was involved in trying to break up the ensuing fight. After re-entering the nightclub immediately after the incident V collapsed and subsequently died of a ruptured renal artery aneurism. The cause of V's death was a rise in blood pressure brought on by his involvement in the affray which led to the rupture of the aneurism. At the close of the prosecution case the judge stopped the trial, ruling that the prosecution would have to prove that V died of the type of harm that a sober and reasonable person would inevitably have realised the affray risked causing and that, taking the evidence at its highest the prosecution had failed to do so.

The prosecution appealed against the judge's ruling and the Court of Appeal held that it was not a requirement of the *Church* test that a reasonable and sober person foresee the "type" of harm suffered by V, it being sufficient that the unlawful act exposed D to a risk of some, albeit not serious harm. In the present case the affray clearly exposed V to the risk of some harm given the level of violence being used. The fact that the actual cause of death was not from the type of harm that may have been foreseen was not relevant to the question of dangerousness.

Mens rea

The required mens rea for constructive manslaughter is the mens rea for the unlawful act. It must be proved that D intended to commit the unlawful act but it is not necessary to prove that D foresaw that the act would cause death.

KEY CASE

DPP v NEWBURY AND JONES (1977)

The two Ds pushed a paving stone over the side of a bridge as a train approached underneath. It crashed through the window of the cab killing the guard. Convicted of manslaughter, the two appealed on the ground that they had not foreseen any harm as a likely result of their actions. Dismissing their appeal, the House of Lords followed the ruling in *Church* and held that where the killing was the result of an unlawful act, the accused was guilty of manslaughter if the act was objectively dangerous. The test was not one of whether the accused recognised the act to be dangerous but whether sober and reasonable people would have recognised the risk of injury to someone. (The report does not mention what the unlawful act was in this case. Since the Ds apparently did not have the mens rea for assault, the unlawful act must presumably have been criminal damage, contrary to the **Criminal Damage Act 1971** s.1(1).)

KEY CASE

DAWSON (1985)

D and others attempted to rob a filling station, wearing masks and carrying a pickaxe handle and an imitation firearm. The 60-year-old attendant pressed the alarm and the attackers fled. The attendant had a severe heart condition and shortly afterwards died of a heart attack. The Court of Appeal quashed D's manslaughter conviction, holding that the test of whether the act was dangerous was an objective one depending on whether a reasonable person would have recognised the risk of some physical harm to the attendant and the reasonable person must be assumed to know only the facts and circumstances as observed by the defendant. The reasonable person would not have known that the attendant had a weak heart. (In another case, it has been held that if the victim's frailty and old age would have been obvious to a reasonable observer, then at that point the unlawful act may become one which a sober and reasonable person would recognise as carrying the risk of some physical harm: *Watson* (1989).)

Cato (1976)

Two drug addicts were unlawfully in possession of heroin. Each prepared for himself a syringe loaded to his own taste which he then got his friend to inject him with. One of them died as a result. The survivor, D, was convicted of two offences: (1) unlawfully and maliciously administering a noxious substance, contrary to **Offences Against the Person Act 1861** s.23 and, (2) manslaughter. His appeal was dismissed. He had committed an unlawful act (administering a noxious substance) which was dangerous and caused the death. If, instead of D injecting V, V injects himself and dies from the drug, the result will normally be very different: see *Kennedy* (below).

Unlawful act must have caused the death

The unlawful act must have caused the death. It does not, however, have to have been specifically aimed at the victim.

Dalby (1982)

D was lawfully in possession of drugs but unlawfully supplied some of them to the deceased who took them in a dangerous quantity. The Court of Appeal quashed D's conviction, holding that D's act had not been aimed at the victim. By this, the Court of Appeal meant that D's unlawful act of supply had not caused the death. See *Goodfellow* and *Kennedy*, below.

Goodfellow (1986)

D set fire to the council house in which he lived. He tried to make it look like a fire bomb in order to persuade the council to rehouse him and his family on the basis that he was homeless. His wife and another were killed in the fire. He appealed against his conviction for manslaughter on the basis that he had aimed his act at the council and had not aimed it at the victims. Dismissing his appeal, the Court of Appeal held that the unlawful act does not have to be aimed at anyone. It simply has to have caused the death. The court dismissed the statement in *Dalby* that the act had to be aimed at the victim, saying that the relevant point in *Dalby* was that the chain of causation must not be broken.

HOMICIDE

147

Use of illegal drugs can lead to death. Where D injects V with the illegal drug and V dies of the injection, D is normally guilty of constructive manslaughter since the injecting of the drugs is an unlawful act (administering a noxious substance and/or supplying a controlled drug), the act is dangerous and has led to the death: see, for example, *Cato*, above. Where D supplies the illegal drug to V and it is V who subsequently injects himself or takes the drug orally and then dies from the drug, it will for two reasons be difficult to convict D of constructive manslaughter. First, the supply of the drug, though an unlawful (and presumably dangerous) act, cannot easily be shown to have been a cause of V's death. V's independent decision to take the drug will normally break the chain of causation: *Kennedy* (below). Secondly, D cannot be said to have been a party to an unlawful act by V, since self-injection or consumption of a controlled drug is not an unlawful act: *Dias* (2002).

KEY CASE

KENNEDY (2007)

D prepared a syringe of heroin ready for immediate use and handed it to V. V injected himself and died as a result. The House of Lords quashed D's conviction for manslaughter. The Court of Appeal had certified a question asking:

> "When is it appropriate to find someone guilty of manslaughter where that person has been involved in the supply of a class A controlled drug, which is then freely and voluntarily self-administered by the person to whom it was supplied, and the administration of the drug then causes his death?"

The answer from the House of Lords was "In the case of a fully-informed and responsible adult, never". The decision by V to take the drug breaks the chain of causation.

In *Butcher* [2011] D's conviction for manslaughter, based on the supply of heroin to V who self-administered the drug, was quashed by the Court of Appeal in light of the House of Lord's decision in *Kennedy*.

Summary of constructive manslaughter

ACTUS REUS *D must:*	● Commit an unlawful act; ● which is dangerous; and ● which causes death.

MENS REA *D must possess:*	● The intention to commit the unlawful act (there is no requirement that D foresees death).

Manslaughter by gross negligence

In order for D to be liable for manslaughter by gross negligence it must be established that D owed V a duty of care, D breached that duty of care, the breach of duty caused V's death and the breach of duty was "grossly negligent".

Duty of care

Individuals owe no general duty of care to others but a duty of care may exist in certain specified situations. Examples of cases where a duty of care has been imposed include: *Adomako* (1995) (doctors to patients); *Hood* (2003) (close relatives); *Litchfield* (1998) (employers to their employees); *Singh* (1999) (landlords to their tenants) and *Stone and Dobinson* (1977) (where a duty of care has been assumed).

Breach of duty

The standard of care expected of a person who owes a duty of care is a *"fair and reasonable"* standard of care and competence: *Bateman* (1925). In *Adomako* the expected standard of care was expressed as being that of a reasonably competent person performing the activity. The breach of duty must cause the death of V.

Gross negligence

For the negligence to amount to "gross negligence", it must be something which goes beyond the ordinary civil law concept of negligence, to be such that it warrants criminal liability. It is for the jury to decide whether, having regard to risk of death involved, the accused's act (or omission) was so bad in all the circumstances as to be criminal: *Bateman, Adomako*.

KEY CASE

BATEMAN (1925)

D, a doctor, was charged with manslaughter arising out of the death of a patient whose confinement he attended whilst she was giving birth. It was alleged that he was guilty of two aspects of medical negligence and that he had delayed too long in having the patient removed to hospital. He was convicted but appealed successfully to the Court of Criminal Appeal. It was held that the determining factor in manslaughter was the degree of negligence. It had to be more than merely absence of that ordinary care which in the circumstances a prudent person ought to have taken. It has to have been such that it went beyond a mere matter of compensation between subjects and must have shown such disregard for the life and safety of others as to amount to a crime against the state and be deserving of punishment.

KEY CASE

ADOMAKO (1994)

D was the anaesthetist at an eye operation. During the operation the tube from the ventilator supplying oxygen to the patient became disconnected. D failed to notice this for a period of six minutes before the patient suffered a cardiac arrest from which they died. At D's trial for manslaughter, the judge directed the jury that they could convict if they were satisfied that D was guilty of gross negligence. Dismissing D's appeal against conviction, the House of Lords followed the decision in *Bateman* and held that the test for manslaughter was gross negligence.

Their Lordships overruled their own decision in *Seymour* (1983) where it had been held that the test of liability was one based on the *Caldwell* definition of recklessness. They stated that *Caldwell* recklessness is no part of the test, which is one of gross negligence. Their Lordships made it clear that there is no separate offence of "motor manslaughter". If the killing was by means of a vehicle, then, just as where the killing was caused by any other means, the test of liability for manslaughter was one of gross negligence, as stated in *Andrews v DPP*, above.

KEY CASE

MISRA, SRIVASTAVA (2004)

After a surgical operation the patient became infected. The two Ds, senior house doctors responsible for the patient's post-operative care, failed to make an adequate diagnosis of the patient's condition, a severe infection requiring aggressive therapy and antibiotics. As a result he died. They were convicted of manslaughter by gross negligence. Dismissing their appeal, the Court of Appeal held that the definition of the crime is not incompatible with the European Convention on Human Rights art.7, entitled "No Punishment without Law" which requires the law to be certain. The ingredients of the offence were clearly defined by the House of Lords in *Adomako* and involve no uncertainty which offends against art.7. The ingredients are: (i) a negligent breach of a duty of care owed by the defendant to the victim, thereby exposing the victim to the risk of death; (ii) the circumstances were so reprehensible as to amount to gross negligence; (iii) the breach of duty was a substantial cause of the victim's death. There is no additional requirement for the jury to decide whether the defendant's behaviour was a crime. The issue for the jury is not whether the defendant's negligence was gross and whether additionally it is a crime, but whether his behaviour was grossly negligent and consequently criminal.

Summary of gross negligence manslaughter

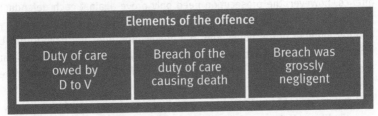

Elements of the offence		
Duty of care owed by D to V	Breach of the duty of care causing death	Breach was grossly negligent

Reckless manslaughter

There is authority for the existence of a separate category of manslaughter, reckless manslaughter, where the defendant is proved to have carried on his actions, being aware that they involved a high probability of death or serious injury to the deceased: *Lidar* (2000). It is perfectly permissible for a judge to use the word "reckless" in the ordinary connotation of that term in describing to the jury the amount of negligence required before it can be found to be "gross": per Lord Mackay in *Adomako*. This does not alter the fact that the test for manslaughter by gross negligence is entirely objective, not requiring proof that the defendant himself foresaw any risk of death or injury.

KILLING A CHILD OR VULNERABLE ADULT

The **Domestic Violence, Crime and Victims Act 2004** s.5, created the offence of causing or allowing the death of, or serious physical harm to, a child (someone aged under 16) or a vulnerable adult (someone over 16 "whose ability to protect himself from violence, abuse or neglect is significantly impaired through physical or mental disability or illness, through old age or otherwise"). The maximum punishment is 14 years' imprisonment. The requirements for the offence are:

- The victim (V) died as a result of an unlawful act by a person (whether D or someone else), living in the same household as, and having frequent contact with, V.
- The defendant (D) was such a person.
- At the time of the unlawful act, there was a significant risk of physical harm being caused to V by such a person.

Where the victim (e.g. a child or a senile person) lived in a household with two or more others and has clearly been killed by the unlawful act of one of them, the prosecution may well find itself unable to secure a conviction for manslaughter against any member of the household because it is unable to prove which of them committed the fatal unlawful act. For the present offence, however, the prosecution need only prove against each defendant that the fatal unlawful act was committed either by the defendant or by another member of the household. The prosecution does not have to prove which of these two alternatives was the case. However, if it cannot prove that the defendant (D) committed the fatal act, the prosecution must also prove that:

- D was, or ought to have been, aware of the above risk of serious physical harm being caused to V;
- D failed to such steps as he could reasonably have been expected to take to protect V from the risk; and
- The fatal unlawful act occurred in circumstances of the kind that D foresaw, or ought to have foreseen.

CORPORATE MANSLAUGHTER

The **Corporate Manslaughter and Corporate Homicide Act 2007** created the offence of corporate manslaughter. Section 1(1) provides:

(1) An organisation to which this section applies is guilty of an offence if the way in which its activities are managed or organised—
   (a) causes a person's death, and
   (b) amounts to a gross breach of a relevant duty of care owed by the organisation to the deceased.

This enactment may make it easier to secure convictions for manslaughter against corporations where corporate failings have led to deaths, e.g. on oil rigs, in rail crashes, in prison cells, etc. The organisations which can commit this offence include companies, government departments, police forces and (provided that they are employers) partnerships, trade unions and employers associations. The offence is not committed, however, unless "the way in which the organisation's activities are managed by its senior management is a substantial element" in the gross breach of duty: s.1(3). Thus it is necessary to show failings at a senior level in the organisation, though not necessarily at board level. A gross breach of duty of care amounts to much the same thing as does gross negligence in manslaughter at common law. The relevant duties of care include all of the following: duties owed to the organisation's employees and workers, duties owed as occupier and duties owed in connection with any of the following: the supply by the organisation of goods, services, construction and maintenance work, the carrying on by the organisation of any activity on a commercial basis, the use or keeping by the organisation of plant and machinery. Also included are duties owed to those in custody in police stations, prisons and other custodial institutions.

Secondary liability is expressly excluded. Thus no individual can be charged with aiding, abetting, counselling or procuring the offence of corporate manslaughter. In relation to corporations, the statutory offence of corporate manslaughter replaces the common law offence of manslaughter by gross negligence. Thus organisations which can commit the statutory offence can no longer be guilty of the common law offence of manslaughter by gross negligence, though they could still commit the common law offence of manslaughter by an unlawful act.

HOMICIDE

153

KEY CASE

COTSWOLD GEOTECHNICAL HOLDINGS LTD [2011]

Cotswold Geotechnical Holdings Ltd were a company concerned in soil investigation. In order to obtain a soil sample in the course of an investigation a pit was dug to a depth of 3.5 metres. The pit was entirely unsupported and collapsed upon an employee of the company who had entered it to obtain the relevant sample. The employee died of traumatic asphyxia. The company was convicted of corporate manslaughter on the basis that it was in gross breach of its duty of care to the deceased by not enforcing a strict prohibition on entering pits of such depth without ensuring that the proper shoring was in place. A fine of £385,000 was upheld on appeal even though it resulted in the company entering administration.

CAUSING DEATH BY DRIVING

Prompted by the apparent reluctance of juries to convict motorists of manslaughter, Parliament long ago enacted an additional offence, now in **Road Traffic Act 1988** s.1, of causing death by dangerous driving (maximum sentence 14 years' imprisonment). In 1991, s.3A was inserted into the **Road Traffic Act 1988** creating the offence of causing death by *careless driving whilst unfit* through drink or drugs or above the drink/drive alcohol limit (maximum sentence 14 years). The Road Safety Act 2006 inserted a new s.2B into the Road Traffic Act 1988 creating a further offence of causing death by *careless or inconsiderate* driving (maximum sentence five years). The 2006 Act also inserted into s.3ZB of the 1988 Act an offence of causing death by driving whilst unlicensed, disqualified or uninsured. In *Hughes* [2013] the Supreme Court determined that "causing death" in the context of this offence entailed more than mere factual causation and required some element of fault on behalf of D (for a more detailed discussion of this case see Causation in Ch.1).

PROPOSALS FOR REFORM

In its report *Murder, Manslaughter and Infanticide*, Law Com 304 (2006), the Law Commission recommended replacing the current offences of murder and manslaughter with the following graduated series of offences:

1st degree murder (mandatory life sentence)

(a) Killing intentionally, or

(b) Killing where there is an intention to do serious injury coupled with an awareness of a serious risk of causing death.

2nd degree murder (discretionary sentence up to a maximum of life imprisonment)

(a) Killing with an intention to cause serious injury, or

(b) Killing where there is an intention to cause some injury or a fear or risk of injury, coupled with an awareness of a serious risk of causing death, or

(c) Killing reduced from first degree murder by a partial defence (provocation, diminished responsibility or participation in a suicide pact).

Manslaughter (discretionary sentence up to a maximum of life imprisonment)

(a) Killing through gross negligence as to a risk of causing death, or

(b) Killing through a criminal act with either,

    (i) an intention to cause injury or,

    (ii) an awareness of a risk of causing injury, or

(c) Participating in a joint criminal venture in the course of which another participant commits first or second degree murder, in circumstances where the risk of that happening should have been obvious.

The same report recommended allowing *duress* as a defence to first degree and second degree murder and to attempted murder, but subject to two significant qualifications:

(a) the threat must be one of death or life threatening harm, and

(b) the legal burden of proof should be placed on the defendant.

Proposals for reform of the partial defences to murder were made by the Law Commission Report 290 on Partial Defences to Murder (2004). Although not all of the proposals were accepted, the new partial defence to murder of loss of self control and the amendments to the defence of diminished responsibility introduced by the **Coroners and Justice Act 2009** reflect a number of the Law Commission's suggestions.

REVISION CHECKLIST

You should now know and understand:

☐   the required elements of the offence of murder;

☐   the operation of the partial defences to murder of loss of self control, diminished responsibility and suicide pact and the effect of successfully pleading the defences;

☐ the required elements of the offence of constructive manslaughter;

☐ the required elements of the offence of gross negligence manslaughter;

☐ the required elements of the offence of reckless manslaughter;

☐ when liability may be imposed for the killing of a child or vulnerable adult;

☐ when liability for death may be imposed on a corporation;

☐ offences relating to causing death by driving;

☐ proposed reform of the law of homicide.

QUESTION AND ANSWER

QUESTION

Bernadette volunteers to go along on a school outing as extra adult supervision is needed. She is in charge of a small group of girls. At the seaside she sunbathes while they paddle. On hearing a scream she sits up to see two girls, Elizabeth and Jane, out of their depth and drowning. She mistakenly assumes that they are playing and that there is no risk. William, a passer-by dives in and rescues the girls. Overreacting, he gives Elizabeth unnecessary mouth to mouth resuscitation and heart massage. Unknown to him, she has a weak heart, has heart failure and dies. While all this is going on, Jane is ignored and is not seen by Bernadette for several hours. She catches pneumonia due to her exposure, is ill for several months and then dies.

Discuss whether Bernadette and William may be criminally liable for homicide.

ADVICE AND THE ANSWER

Homicide spans a wide range of situations involving unlawful killing from murder at the most serious to involuntary manslaughter which can, in some instances, be only barely distinguishable from accidental death. It is therefore important that you can identify which offence you need to apply.

Where you have a defendant who intends to kill or cause serious harm you will need to consider murder. This may mean you also need to consider the special partial defences to murder, loss of self control, diminished responsibility and suicide pact where the circumstances of the case give rise to the possibility. Remember that successfully pleading any of these defences will reduce the liability of the defendant to (voluntary) manslaughter.

Where the defendant does not intend to kill or cause serious harm you will need to consider the possibility of constructive manslaughter. This can take three forms. Constructive or unlawful and dangerous act manslaughter should be considered where D has committed an unlawful act which is objectively dangerous (i.e. carries with it the risk of causing some, albeit not serious, harm). Gross negligence manslaughter arises where D owes V a duty of care, D breaches the duty of care which causes V's death and D is grossly (criminally) negligent. Finally where D foresees a risk of death or serious injury but goes on to take that risk D could be liable for reckless manslaughter.

Another issue which you will often need to consider is the issue of causation (a detailed discussion of causation can be found in Ch.1).

It is important that you establish causation as, if D did not cause the death of V, D cannot be held liable for V's death.

Answer plan

1 The legal issues raised by this question appear to be liability for omissions, unlawful act manslaughter, manslaughter by gross negligence, causation.

2 Bernadette has voluntarily undertaken responsibility (assumed a duty of care), she may be liable for omitting to act. *Stone and Dobinson.*

3 Elizabeth's death. She omits to act when she should. Was she grossly negligent, how is this defined (*Adomako, Misra*)? Was death foreseeable? Question for the jury: "Having regard to risk of death, was Bernadette's failure to act so bad in the circumstances as to merit punishment as manslaughter?" *Adomako, Bateman.*

4 Was B's omission a substantial cause of death or was W's action an intervening act which breaks the chain? *Pagett, Malcherek.* Was her omission still a significant cause despite the new act? Is victim's weak heart relevant? *Blaue.*

5 Does W's treatment constitute negligent medical treatment, and if so, does it make a difference? *Cheshire.*

6 Jane's death. Omission to care for girl. (See above.)

7 Gross negligence, reasonable standard, foreseeability of death, *Adomako.* (See above.)

8 Causation, not insignificant *Hughes* (or significant *Cheshire*) cause of death. (See above.)

9 William's act has, apparently caused Elizabeth's death. Has he committed an unlawful act? An assault? Offences Against the Person Act 1861. *Savage.*

10 Dangerous? Was there an obvious risk of some physical injury, albeit not serious harm? *Church.*

11 William did not know of the weak heart. Would the reasonable man have known? *Dawson.*

12 Is William's act a cause of death? *Pagett.*

13 Was William grossly negligent? (See above.)

Offences against property **10**

INTRODUCTION

There are two main types of offence against property, namely dishonesty offences and offences involving damage. The key dishonesty offences are theft, handling stolen goods, burglary, robbery and blackmail, which are all offences under the **Theft Act 1968**. (Fraud will be dealt with in Ch.11.) The main offences concerning damage are criminal damage, aggravated criminal damage, and arson, which are contained in the **Criminal Damage Act 1971**. As will be seen, these two Acts use similar terminology and similar definitions.

THEFT

LEGISLATION HIGHLIGHTER

Section 1(1) of the **Theft Act 1968** provides that "a person is guilty of theft if he dishonestly appropriates property belonging to another with the intention of permanently depriving the other of it." Sections 2–6 of the 1968 Act supply explanations and definitions of the elements of theft.

Actus reus
The actus reus of theft consists of the act of appropriation of property and the circumstance that the property belongs to another.

Appropriation
Section 3(1) of the 1968 Act states that "any assumption by a person of the rights of an owner amounts to an appropriation ..."

This definition is extremely wide and is not limited to simply taking property. The courts have held that appropriation occurs in a variety of other situations, such as destroying property or selling it.

KEY CASE

MORRIS (1984)

D1 removed price labels from items in a supermarket and attached them to more expensive items. He took these items to the checkout and paid the lower price. In the conjoined appeal of *Anderton v Burnside*, D2 also switched the labels on goods in a supermarket. In this case, however, his actions were discovered before he paid for them. Both Ds were convicted of theft. The House of Lords ruled that the assumption of any of the rights of an owner constituted appropriation. D need not assume *all* of the owner's rights. Theft was committed at the moment that D1 and D2 switched the labels.

Furthermore, under s.3(1), where a person has come by property without stealing it, a later assumption of a right can be an appropriation, e.g. by dishonestly keeping it after it should have been returned.

Appropriation and consent

One issue that has arisen is whether an act amounts to appropriation if it is done with the owner's consent. The House of Lords' decisions in *Lawrence* (1971) and *Morris* (1984) (see above) are difficult to reconcile in this regard. In *Lawrence* the House of Lords decided that D had appropriated property even though the owner consented to him taking it. However, in an obiter comment in *Morris,* Lord Roskill stated that appropriation "involves not an act expressly or impliedly authorised by the owner but an act by way of adverse interference with or usurpation of [an owner's] rights." The issue was finally resolved by the House of Lords in *Gomez* (1992).

KEY CASE

DPP v GOMEZ (1992)

D dishonestly persuaded his employer to accept what D knew to be a worthless cheque in payment for some electrical goods. The employer consented to D handing over the goods to the fraudster presenting the cheque. D was convicted of theft of the goods and appealed. He argued that there had been no appropriation because the owner had consented to him supplying the goods. Their Lordships ruled that an act may be an appropriation notwithstanding that it is done with the consent of the owner. D had, therefore, appropriated the goods when he supplied them to the fraudster.

NB: *Morris* remains good law insofar as it confirms that the assumption of any one or more of the rights of an owner constitutes appropriation.

The courts have even held that a person who receives a gift can be said to have appropriated the property she receives. In *Hinks* (2001), D became friendly with a man of limited intelligence. She influenced him to withdraw sums totalling £60,000 from his building society, which D deposited in her own bank account. Her defence was that they were gifts or loans. She was convicted of theft and appealed, arguing that there could be no appropriation (and, consequently, no theft) where there had been a valid gift or a valid transfer of ownership to a defendant. The House of Lords rejected that argument as inconsistent with the decisions in *Lawrence* and *Gomez* and dismissed her appeal.

Continuing appropriation

The duration of theft can be important for a number of reasons, including:

(i) The offence of handling stolen property can only be committed "otherwise than in the course of stealing".

(ii) For the offence of robbery, theft must be accompanied, or immediately preceded, by the use or threat of force. If the theft is complete before any force is used or threatened, there can be no robbery.

(iii) Goods which have once been stolen cannot be stolen again by the same thief exercising the same, or other, rights of ownership over them.

In *Atakpu and Abrahams* (1994), the Court of Appeal ruled that "appropriation can continue for so long as the thief can sensibly be regarded as in the act of stealing or, in more understandable words, so long as he is 'on the job'".

KEY CASE

ATAKPU AND ABRAHAMS (1994)

Two Ds appealed against convictions for theft. They had hired cars in Germany using false documents, intending to bring them to England to sell them. They were arrested after the cars arrived at Dover and charged with conspiracy to steal. They argued that the cars had been appropriated in Germany and that the theft had, therefore, occurred outside the jurisdiction. The prosecution argued that appropriation was a continuing act and that the defendants were still stealing at the time of their arrival in England. The Court of Appeal accepted that appropriation could be a continuing concept. However, in this case the appropriation occurred when the cars were hired in Germany. It could not be said that it was still continuing several days later when the defendants brought the cars to England to dispose of.

Conversely, in *Hale* (see below), it was held that appropriation was still continuing when two robbers stole some jewellery and then used force in order to escape.

Property

Property is defined by s.4(1) to include money and all real or personal property, including things in action and other intangible property, such as credit in a bank account. This wide definition means that property even encompasses items which it is unlawful to possess, such as proscribed drugs: *Smith* (2011)

Real property means land and buildings, whereas personal property includes movable items. A thing in action means a right in property which can be claimed or enforced by legal action, such as a credit balance in a bank account. To cause a reduction in the size of V's bank account is to appropriate a thing in action belonging to V (namely V's right to claim the relevant amount from the bank). For example, in *Williams (Roy)* (2000), D was a builder who dishonestly over-billed for work which he had done. In payment, D received from V a cheque which D paid into his account. This was a genuine cheque but it had been obtained dishonestly. By paying it into his account, D dishonestly appropriated part of the credit in V's bank account. D was guilty of theft of that amount of credit from V's bank account.

If D causes V's bank account to be debited, he has appropriated property. This is so even if the bank is bound to replenish the account: *Hilton* (1997). There will be no theft, however, unless, at the time of the dishonest withdrawal, either the account was in credit or else the debit balance was within an authorised overdraft limit: *Kohn* (1979).

Sections 4(2)–(4) specify that certain types of property cannot be stolen. Under s.4(2), land cannot be stolen, although things severed from land can be stolen. Under s.4(3), wild mushrooms and plants cannot be stolen unless they are picked for a commercial purpose. Under s.4(4), a wild animal that is not tamed or ordinarily kept in captivity cannot be stolen unless it has been, or is in the process of being, reduced into possession. This means that, for example, it would not be theft to take a wild deer but it would be theft to take a deer from a zoo.

Other intangible property included an export quota in *Attorney General of Hong Kong v Nai Keung* (1987). However, the courts have decided that electricity is not intangible property within the meaning of s.4: *Low v Blease* (1975) (although there is a separate offence of abstracting electricity under s.13 of the 1968 Act). Furthermore, in *Oxford v Moss* (1979), the Divisional Court held that confidential information was not property. Thus, a student who took an exam paper and memorised the questions before replacing it, could not be guilty of stealing the examination questions. (He could not be guilty of stealing the paper itself because he always intended to put it back and there was, accordingly, no intention to permanently deprive—see below.)

Belonging to another

For the actus reus of theft to be complete, the property must belong to another person at the time of the appropriation. Under s.5(1), property is regarded as belonging to anyone having possession or control of it or having a proprietary right or interest in it.

The courts have interpreted the phrase "possession or control" liberally.

KEY CASE

Turner No. 2 (1971) demonstrates that it is possible for D to be convicted of theft of his own property. D had taken his car to a garage to be repaired. He later used a spare key to take the car from where it was parked, without paying for the repairs. The Court of Appeal held that the car "belonged to" the repairer at the time D took it as the repairer had possession or control of it. D was, therefore, guilty of theft.

A person can be in control of property even if he is unaware of that fact. In *Woodman* (1974), D stole scrap metal from a disused factory. The owner of the factory (V) had sold all of the scrap metal on the site to a third party. V was not aware that some of the scrap metal had been left behind. The Court of Appeal held that the scrap metal was under V's control even though V was unaware of its existence. D's conviction for theft of property belonging to V was upheld.

The phrase "proprietary right or interest" is also wider than ownership. It includes those who have an equitable interest in property, such as beneficiaries under a trust. It also includes co-owners of property. Thus, where D and V are co-owners of property, D may be liable for theft from V if he appropriates that property: *Bonner* (1970).

Lost property still belongs to its owner and can be stolen. Property that has been abandoned no longer belongs to another and cannot be stolen. However, the courts will not readily infer abandonment. In *R (Ricketts) v Basildon Magistrates' Court* (2011), D was charged with the theft of bags of clothing that had been left outside charity shops. The court held that the clothing was not abandoned property. A person who donates clothing to a charity shop remains the owner of the property until the charity shop takes possession of it.

There are some circumstances where legal ownership, possession and control have all passed to the defendant but, for the purposes of the Theft

Act, the property is treated as still belonging to the original owner. Section 5(3) states:

> "Where a person receives property from or on account of another, and is under an obligation to the other to retain and deal with that property or its proceeds in a particular way, the property or proceeds shall be regarded (as against him) as belonging to the other."

This subsection is relevant only where ownership of the goods has passed to D. It is mainly concerned with money given to D on the understanding that he will deal with it in a particular way.

KEY CASE

DAVIDGE V BUNNETT (1984)

D's flatmates gave D money to pay certain household bills. D spent the proceeds on Christmas presents. The Divisional Court upheld her conviction for theft on the ground that she was under a legal obligation to use the money in a particular way. The money was, therefore, property belonging to another by virtue of s.5(3).

A different view was taken in *Hall* (1973). In that case D was a travel agent who had taken money from customers but failed to book their holidays. D had paid the money into his general business account. His business then collapsed before the holidays were purchased, and the money was lost. The Court of Appeal held that, although D had a general obligation to fulfil his contract, he did not have to deal with those specific notes and cheques in a particular way. For example, he did not have to keep a separate account with that money in it. Accordingly, s.5(3) did not apply and the property did not belong to another at the time of the appropriation.

Conversely, in *Klineberg and Marsden* (1998), a number of convictions were upheld on the ground that s.5(3) applied. D1 was the director of a company which sold timeshares and D2 was in charge of the company's London office. Purchasers of timeshares paid D1 and D2 on the understanding that the money they paid would be transferred immediately to a trustee to hold until the timeshare apartments were built. The money never reached the trustee. The Court of Appeal held that because D1 and D2 had been obliged to deal with the money in a specific way, it was to be regarded as belonging to the purchasers by virtue of s.5(3).

Section 5(4) sets out a further situation in which property is to be treated as belonging to the original owner, even though possession, control and ownership have passed to D:

> "Where a person gets property by another's mistake, and is under an obligation to make restoration (in whole or in part) of the property or its proceeds or of the value thereof, then to the extent of that obligation the property or proceeds shall be regarded (as against him) as belonging to the person entitled to restoration ...".

Where D obtains property by another's mistake and is under a duty to restore it (or its value), s.5(4) provides that it is to be treated as property belonging to another.

KEY CASE

In *Attorney-General's Reference No.1 of 1983*, D was a police officer who was mistakenly paid £74 in wages for work she had not done. When she found out she did nothing. It was held that s.5(4) applied because she was under an obligation to make restoration of the money. If she dishonestly decided not to repay it, she was guilty of theft.

For s.5(4) to apply, an obligation to repay must be a legal obligation and not merely a moral or social one: *Gilks* (1972).

However, it appears that reliance on s.5(4) will not always be necessary. In *Shadrokh-Cigari* (1988), D was the guardian of a minor. Funds for the minor were transferred from an American to an English bank, but the American bank over-credited the account. D persuaded the minor to sign banker's drafts credited to D. D then spent most of the excess money before the error was discovered. He was convicted of theft, and appealed. His appeal was dismissed. The court held that there were two routes to a conviction. Under s.5(4), he had obtained property by another's mistake, and was, therefore, liable. Alternatively, the fact that the bank had made a mistake meant that the bank retained an equitable interest in the drafts. Accordingly, the situation was covered by s.5(1) and s.5(4) was not really necessary.

Mens rea

There are two elements of mens rea in theft: dishonesty and intention to deprive permanently.

Dishonesty

The 1968 Act does not define dishonesty. Rather, s.2(1) of the Act sets out three situations in which, as a matter of law, a person is *not* dishonest:

(a) Where he believes he has a right in law to deprive the owner of the property.

(b) Where he believes that the owner would consent to the appropriation if he knew of the appropriation and the circumstances of it.

(c) Where he believes that the owner cannot be discovered by taking reasonable steps.

Section 2(2) specifically states that a person can be found to be dishonest notwithstanding his willingness to pay for the property.

D is *not* dishonest if he believes in any one of the things set out in s.2(1). All that is required is a genuine and honest belief; D's belief need not be correct or even reasonable.

In situations not covered by s.2(1), whether D was dishonest remains a question of fact for the jury to decide. Early cases under the Act suggested that there was no need to define dishonesty, which was an ordinary word in the English language and easily understood. In *Feely* (1973), the Court of Appeal agreed that dishonesty was a word in common use, but held that jurors should "apply the current standards of ordinary decent people." This evolved into the *Ghosh* test.

KEY CASE

GHOSH (1982)

D was a doctor acting as a locum consultant at a hospital. He claimed fees for an operation he had not carried out but maintained that he was not dishonest because he was owed that amount in consultation fees. The Court of Appeal dismissed his appeal against his conviction for theft and laid down a two stage test for determining whether a person is dishonest:

(i) The jury must decide if D's behaviour was dishonest by the ordinary standards of reasonable and honest people. If it was *not*, he is not guilty.

(ii) If his behaviour *was* dishonest by the ordinary standards of reasonable and honest people, D is nevertheless not dishonest unless he realised that his behaviour was dishonest by those standards.

The *Ghosh* test is a hybrid test. The first limb of the test is objective and involves measuring D's conduct against an external standard. The second limb of the test is subjective and requires an assessment of D's state of mind. Lord Lane C.J. explained that a hybrid test was necessary to avoid a defendant incurring liability in a situation to which "no moral obloquy could possibly attach." He gave the following example:

> "[A] man... comes from a country where public transport is free. On his first day here he travels on a bus. He gets off without paying. He never had any intention of paying. His mind is clearly honest; but his conduct, judged objectively by what he has done, is dishonest."

Under the *Ghosh* test, the man would not be dishonest in this situation.

Nevertheless, the *Ghosh* test has been the subject of academic criticism. One problem with the test is that there is no single universal standard of dishonesty. There is, therefore, a risk of inconsistency between verdicts, with different juries coming to different decisions in similar cases. The case of *DPP v Gohill* (2007) is an example of this. D was an employee of a tool hire company who altered records to allow regular customers to obtain free hire. In return, D received tips of £5 and £10. He argued that his actions had been intended to enhance the business by keeping customers happy. The magistrates who originally tried him found that his conduct was not dishonest by ordinary standards and acquitted him. The Divisional Court disagreed and allowed the prosecution's appeal against D's acquittal. This case is an example of different courts coming to different conclusions about whether reasonable and honest people would regard D's behaviour as dishonest.

Dishonesty

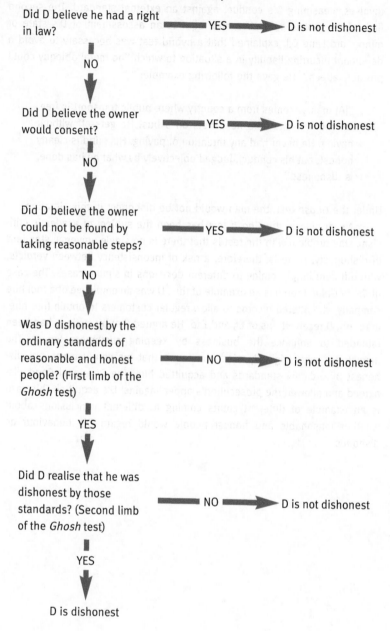

Did D believe he had a right in law? ━━━YES━━━▶ D is not dishonest

NO

Did D believe the owner would consent? ━━━YES━━━▶ D is not dishonest

NO

Did D believe the owner could not be found by taking reasonable steps? ━━━YES━━━▶ D is not dishonest

NO

Was D dishonest by the ordinary standards of reasonable and honest people? (First limb of the *Ghosh* test) ━━━NO━━━▶ D is not dishonest

YES

Did D realise that he was dishonest by those standards? (Second limb of the *Ghosh* test) ━━━NO━━━▶ D is not dishonest

YES

D is dishonest

Intention to permanently deprive

The defendant must intend to permanently deprive the owner of the property at the time of the appropriation for theft to be complete. Under s.6(2), a defendant intends to permanently deprive another of his property if he intends "to treat the thing as his own to dispose of regardless of the other's rights."

The courts have rejected the dictionary definition of "to dispose of" as being too narrow. In *DPP v Lavender* (1994), the Divisional Court held that disposing of something included "dealing" with it.

In *Marshall, Coombes and Eren* (1998), three Ds obtained travel tickets from members of the public leaving the London Underground and re-sold them to other potential customers. The Ds were convicted of theft of the tickets. They appealed, claiming they had not intended to deprive London Underground of the tickets permanently, since the tickets would be returned to London Underground when used by the purchasers. The Court of Appeal held that by acquiring and re-selling the tickets, the Ds were treating them as their own to dispose of regardless of the rights of London Underground. Their appeals were dismissed.

A defendant can be said to intend to permanently deprive even if he intends to replace the property he has appropriated with property of equivalent value. For example, in *Velumyl* (1989), D took some money from his company's safe to loan to a friend. He intended to replace it when his friend paid him back. The Court of Appeal upheld his conviction for theft on the basis that he clearly intended to deprive the owner of the specific banknotes he had taken. An intention to replace them with banknotes of equivalent value was insufficient.

Borrowing or lending

Section 6(2) goes on to state that a person who borrows or lends another's property can be regarded as intending to permanently deprive the other of it, "but only if... the borrowing or lending is for a period and in such circumstances making it equivalent to an outright taking or disposal."

KEY CASE

In Lloyd (1985), D was a cinema projectionist who borrowed films and gave them to another man to copy, before returning them to the cinema. The Court of Appeal held that "a mere borrowing is never enough to constitute the necessary guilty mind unless the intention is to return the 'thing' in such a changed state that it can truly be said that all its goodness or virtue has gone." D's appeal against his conviction for theft was allowed.

Conversely, in *Raphael* (2008), two Ds were convicted of theft after taking V's car and offering to sell it back to him. The Court of Appeal held that, by offering to sell V's own property back to him, the defendants had treated it as their own to dispose of regardless of V's rights.

Conditional intent to permanently deprive

The case of *Easom* (1971) confirmed that a defendant will not be liable for theft if he only has a conditional intention to deprive the owner permanently. D picked up a woman's handbag and looked through it. Finding nothing of interest, he replaced the bag and all of its contents. He was convicted of theft of the bag. His conviction was quashed on appeal on the basis that a condition intention, i.e. an intention to steal *if* he found anything of value, was not sufficient. (If properly charged, he could on those facts be convicted of attempted theft—see attempting the impossible, p.57, above.)

SUMMARY OF THEFT

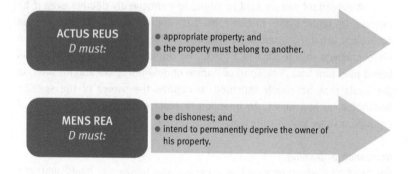

ACTUS REUS
D must:
- appropriate property; and
- the property must belong to another.

MENS REA
D must:
- be dishonest; and
- intend to permanently deprive the owner of his property.

HANDLING STOLEN GOODS

Section 22 of the 1968 Act provides that a person is guilty of handling stolen goods if, knowing or believing them to be stolen, and acting other than in the course of stealing, he dishonestly does one of the following:

(i) Receives the goods.
(ii) Arranges to receive them.
(iii) Undertakes their retention, removal, disposal or realisation.
(iv) Arranges to undertake the above.
(v) Assists in their retention, removal, disposal or realisation.
(vi) Arranges to assist the above.

Except where the form of the offence is receiving the goods (or arranging to receive them), the offence is committed only if the defendant acted by or for the benefit of another.

Actus reus

Stolen goods

The goods must have been stolen at the time the handling offence is alleged to have been committed. If the defendant is alleged to have committed the offence by "arranging" to receive or "arranging" to assist, then the goods must already have been stolen at the time the arrangement was made: *Park* (1988).

Goods are stolen goods if they were obtained by theft (and, therefore, also by robbery or burglary), by blackmail, or by fraud: s.24(4). Under s.24(3), they cease to be stolen goods after they have been restored to the person from whom they were stolen or to other lawful possession or custody (e.g. that of the police). They also cease to be stolen goods after the person from whom they were stolen ceases to have a right to restitution of them.

KEY CASE

In **Attorney-General's Reference No.1 of 1974**, a constable saw an unlocked, unattended car containing goods which he correctly suspected had been stolen. He removed the rotor arm from the car to immobilise it and waited nearby. When D appeared and tried to start the car, the constable questioned and then arrested him. The trial judge directed the jury to acquit D of handling stolen goods on the ground that the goods had been restored to the constable's lawful possession. The Court of Appeal held that the goods were to be regarded as returned to lawful possession only if the constable had assumed control over them, which depended upon whether he *intended* to take them into his custody. If his only object in immobilising the car was to ensure that the driver could not drive away before being questioned, then the goods were not reduced into his possession or control. The issue of the constable's intention should have been left for the jury to decide.

Section 24(2) extends the definition of stolen goods to include any other goods which directly or indirectly represent the stolen goods as being the proceeds of their realisation or disposal. For example, if D sells stolen goods, the proceeds of the sale are also stolen goods.

By or for the benefit of another

Unless the charge is receiving or arranging to receive stolen goods, the defendant must have acted by or for the benefit of another. This distinguishes handlers from thieves who are merely disposing of the goods they have stolen. The thief who keeps or sells property that he has stolen is not guilty of handling because he is acting for his own benefit and not for the benefit of another.

A person who comes by stolen property innocently is not liable if he later becomes aware that it is stolen and retains it or sells it solely for his own benefit: *Bloxham* (1983). However, if he retains the property on behalf of another, he will be liable. In *Pitchley* (1973), D's son gave D some money to look after for him. D was not aware that it was stolen and paid it into his own savings account. D later became aware that it was stolen but nevertheless kept the money on behalf of his son. It was held that he had been properly convicted because he had retained the money for the benefit of his son.

If a defendant knows that goods are stolen and allows them to be stored in his house to assist the thief, he will be guilty of handling. This is because he has assisted in their retention by another, e.g. *Brown* (1969). In *Kanwar* (1982), D lied to police to protect her husband who had brought stolen goods into the house. She falsely claimed that the goods were hers. The Court of Appeal held that she was guilty of handling because her lies were designed to assist in the retention of the stolen goods for the benefit of her husband.

Otherwise than in the course of the stealing

It is a question of fact as to whether the theft is complete. If it is not, the continuation of the stealing cannot be handling. For other reasons why it may matter whether the theft has been completed, see *Atakpu* (above) and *Hale* (below).

Mens rea

The defendant must be dishonest and must know or believe that the goods are stolen.

"Dishonesty" is defined using the *Ghosh* test (see p.166).

The test of "knowledge or belief" is entirely subjective and is not about what the defendant *ought* to have known. In *Atwal v Massey* (1971), the Divisional Court allowed D's appeal against conviction for handling on the grounds that the magistrates had applied the wrong test:

> "If when the justices said that the appellant ought to have known that the [goods were] stolen they meant that any reasonable man would have realised that [they were] stolen, then that was not the

right test. It is not sufficient to establish an offence under section 22 that the goods were received in circumstances which would have put a reasonable man on his enquiry."

Suspicion does not amount to knowledge or belief: *Grainge* (1974); *Forsyth* (1997). Similarly, "deliberately shutting one's eyes to the obvious" is not equivalent to belief: *Moys* (1984); *Forsyth* (1997). However, these cases confirm that a jury is entitled to take into account a defendant's suspicions and whether he shut his eyes to the obvious in deciding whether actual knowledge or belief existed.

ROBBERY

LEGISLATION HIGHLIGHTER

Under s.8(1) of the 1968 Act:

"A person is guilty of robbery if he steals, and immediately before or at the time of doing so and in order to do so, he uses force on any person or puts or seeks to put any person in fear of being then and there subjected to force."

Context

Robbery is an aggravated form of theft. What turns theft into robbery is the use of force, or putting or seeking to put someone in fear of force. The use or threat of force must be immediately before or at the time of stealing and in order to steal.

Theft

If there is no theft, there can be no robbery. So if a defendant is not liable for theft, for example because he was not dishonest, he cannot be liable for robbery either: *Robinson* (1977). Conversely, where D uses or threatens force at the requisite time and all of the other elements of theft are present, there is a robbery as soon as the appropriation takes place. In *Corcoran v Anderton* (1980) two youths agreed to steal a woman's handbag. D1 struck V in the back and tugged at her bag, causing it to fall to the ground. V screamed and both youths ran off empty handed. The Divisional Court held that D1 had appropriated the bag by tugging on it and the defendants had been properly convicted of robbery. It was irrelevant that they did not get away with the property.

Use or threat of force

The force used or threatened must be against a person and not against property. Whether something amounts to force is a question of fact for the jury. In *Dawson* (1976), the Court of Appeal held that nudging a person so that he lost his balance could amount to force.

KEY CASE

In **CLOUDEN** (1987), D wrenched V's shopping bag from her hand. The Court of Appeal held that this was the use of force against V and not just against the bag. D's conviction for robbery was upheld.

Conversely, in *P v DPP* (2012), the Divisional Court held that D had not used force when he snatched a cigarette from V's fingers. Only minimal force had been used to take the cigarette and there had been no physical contact between D and V. The situation was more akin to pickpocketing, which is theft rather than robbery.

Where force is threatened rather than actually used, a defendant will be liable if he either puts another person in fear of force or if he seeks to do so. It does not matter whether the other person in fact fears force: *B and R v DPP* (2007).

Furthermore, force need not be used or threatened against the person from whom the property is stolen. The use or threat of force against any person will suffice.

Immediately before or at the time of stealing

Robbery is not committed if the force is used or threatened after the theft is finished. The issue of when the theft is complete is a question of fact for the jury to decide.

KEY CASE

In **HALE** (1979), D1 and D2 forced their way into V's home. D1 put his hand over V's mouth and D2 went upstairs and returned with a jewellery box. Before leaving, both Ds tied V up to prevent her calling the police. The Court of Appeal held that force had been used immediately before the theft when D1 put his hand over V's mouth. Alternatively, theft was a continuing offence and the jury were entitled to conclude that tying V up in order to escape was the use of force at the time of stealing.

The case of *Hale* was decided before the House of Lords decision in *Gomez* (above). In *Lockley* (1995) D and others took beer from an off licence and, when approached by the shop keeper, used violence towards him. They argued, using *Gomez*, that the theft was complete before violence was used. Dismissing their appeals against convictions for robbery, the Court of Appeal held that *Hale* still applied and it was up to the jury to decide whether the theft was still continuing at the time force was used. (For other decisions on the duration of theft, see *Atakpu* (above).)

In order to steal

Force must be used or threatened in order to steal. For example, if D assaults V and decides afterwards to take V's mobile telephone, D is not liable for robbery.

BURGLARY

> **LEGISLATION HIGHLIGHTER**
>
> Under s.9(1) of the 1968 Act burglary is committed if either:
> (a) D enters any building or part of a building as a trespasser and with intent to commit theft, grievous bodily harm or unlawful damage (s.9(1)(a)); or
> (b) having entered the premises as a trespasser, D steals or attempts to steal, or inflicts or attempts to inflict grievous bodily harm (s.9(1)(b)).

Both types of burglary require the defendant to have entered a building or part of a building as a trespasser.

Entry

The actus reus of burglary requires an entry. The Court of Appeal has said that entry must be "effective and substantial" for burglary to be made out: *Collins* (1972). This was qualified by later cases.

> **KEY CASE**
>
> In **BROWN** (1985), D was seen with the top half of his body inside a broken shop window and his feet still on the ground outside, whilst he rummaged through goods inside. His entry was clearly "effective" and it was held that this was sufficient.

In *Ryan* (1996), D was found trapped with his head and arm inside the window of a house and the rest of his body outside. Following *Brown*, the

Court of Appeal held that partial entry was capable of constituting entry and the fact that D was incapable of stealing anything was irrelevant.

Building or part of a building

The Act does not define "building", although s.9(4) specifically extends it to inhabited vehicles or vessels. It appears that for a structure to constitute a building, some degree of permanence is required: *B and S v Leathley* (1979).

The meaning of "part of a building" was considered in *Walkington* (1979). D entered a department store and then entered the area behind a three-sided counter, where a till was unattended. He looked inside the till, intending to steal from it (although in fact it was empty). His conviction for burglary was upheld on the grounds that he had entered part of a building as a trespasser by going behind the counter.

Trespasser

This essentially means entry with neither a legal right of entry, nor the permission of the occupier. Entry in excess of permission given will also be entry as a trespasser.

KEY CASE

In **JONES AND SMITH (1976)**, S had general permission from his father to enter his father's house. S and J both entered the house intending to steal from inside. It was held that they were both guilty of burglary. S had entered in excess of the permission given, since clearly that permission did not extend to any entry in order to steal.

Trespass also requires mens rea on the part of a defendant. A person only enters as a trespasser if he intends or is subjectively reckless as to whether he is trespassing: *Collins* (1972).

Section 9(1)(a)

For s.9(1)(a) burglary, in addition to the above three elements, the defendant must intend to commit a further specified offence at the time of entry. For the purposes of s.9(1)(a), these offences are theft, grievous bodily harm, or criminal damage: s.9(2). It is immaterial whether the defendant in fact goes on to commit the offence.

Section 9(1)(b)

For section 9(1)(b) burglary, the defendant does not need to have intended to commit an offence at the time of entering the premises (although he may have so intended). Section 9(1)(b) burglary is committed if, having entered a building or part of a building as a trespasser, D goes on to commit theft, attempted theft, grievous bodily harm, or attempted grievous bodily harm.

SUMMARY OF BURGLARY

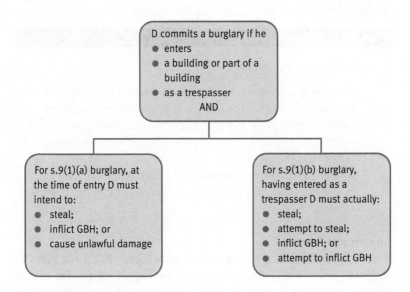

D commits a burglary if he
- enters
- a building or part of a building
- as a trespasser
AND

For s.9(1)(a) burglary, at the time of entry D must intend to:
- steal;
- inflict GBH; or
- cause unlawful damage

For s.9(1)(b) burglary, having entered as a trespasser D must actually:
- steal;
- attempt to steal;
- inflict GBH; or
- attempt to inflict GBH

AGGRAVATED BURGLARY

By s.10 of the 1968 Act, aggravated burglary is committed if a burglar has with him a firearm, imitation firearm, offensive weapon or explosive. Imitation firearm would include a toy gun. An offensive weapon is any article made, adapted or intended to cause injury or to incapacitate a person.

The section does not require any intent to use the weapon, except where it is only an offensive weapon by reason of the defendant's intention to use it to cause injury or to incapacitate. Even then, however, it is enough if he intends to use it should the need arise; he does not have to intend to use it during the course of the burglary. In *Stones* (1989), D had with him an ordinary kitchen knife. He intended to use it to defend himself if he was attacked by a gang, although not necessarily during the burglary he committed. The Court of Appeal held that this was sufficient for liability.

Where the aggravated offence is founded upon s.9(1)(a) burglary, the defendant must have the weapon with him at the time of entry in order to be liable for the aggravated offence. Where the aggravated offence is based upon s.9(1)(b) burglary, the defendant must have the weapon with him when he steals or inflicts grievous bodily harm, or attempts either offence: *Francis* (1982).

BLACKMAIL

LEGISLATION HIGHLIGHTER

Under s.21(1) of the 1968 Act:

"A person is guilty of blackmail if, with a view to gain for himself or another or with intent to cause loss to another, he makes any unwarranted demand with menaces; and for this purpose a demand with menaces is unwarranted unless the person making it does so in the belief—

(a) that he has reasonable grounds for making the demand; and

(b) that the use of the menaces is a proper means of reinforcing the demand."

Unwarranted demand

A demand is made when it is spoken or posted, even if it is not heard or received: *Treacy* (1971). According to the wording of s.21(1), the test of whether a demand is unwarranted is subjective; whether a demand is unwarranted is dependent on the belief of the defendant when he makes the demand.

With a view to gain or intent to cause loss

Under s.34, the gain or loss must involve money or other property, and can be either temporary or permanent. "Gain" includes keeping what one has and "loss" includes not getting what one otherwise might get. There may be a view to gain even if D is seeking to recover that to which he is legally entitled, such as repayment of a debt: *Lawrence and Pomroy* (1971).

Menaces

The word "menaces" has been interpreted widely and is not limited to threats of violence.

Menaces includes "threats of any action detrimental to or unpleasant to the person addressed" (*Thorne v Motor Trade Association* (1937)). The menaces must be "of such a nature and extent that the mind of an ordinary person of normal stability and courage might be influenced or made apprehensive so as to accede unwillingly to the demand" (*Clear* (1968)).

The jury must consider what effect the menaces would have on a normal person. Thus, D may be liable even if V is not actually affected. However, where a person of normal stability would not be influenced by the menaces but V is, D will be liable if he was aware of the likely effect of his actions on V.

In *Harry* (1974), D was a treasurer of a student RAG committee who sent letters to 115 shopkeepers asking them to buy indemnity posters costing between £1 and £5 "to protect you from any Rag Activity...". Fewer than six shopkeepers complained. The trial judge ruled that the reaction of the recipients of the letter could be a guide to the effect the menaces would have had on a person of normal stability. On this basis he found that there was insufficient evidence that menaces had been used and directed the jury to acquit.

The effect of s.21(2) is that the menaces may relate to action to be taken by others. For example, D may threaten that his employees will hurt V unless V complies with D's demands. Furthermore, it is not a requirement that D be in a position to actually carry out the threats, either by his own actions or by the actions of another: *Lambert* (2010).

. . . .

CRIMINAL DAMAGE

Criminal damage offences are covered by a separate Act of Parliament: the **Criminal Damage Act 1971**.

Context
The **Criminal Damage Act 1971** was based the Law Commission's Report, *Offences of Damage to Property* (Law Com No.29, 1970). The Act uses a number of terms that are also used in the **Theft Act 1968** and the Law Commission was keen to promote consistency across both statutes. Accordingly, some of the definitions used in the 1971 Act are similar, although not identical, to the definitions used in the 1968 Act.

LEGISLATION HIGHLIGHTER

Under s.1(1) of the 1971 Act:

"A person who without lawful excuse destroys or damages any property belonging to another intending to destroy or damage any such property or being reckless as to whether any such property would be destroyed or damaged shall be guilty of an offence."

This is often referred to as simple criminal damage to distinguish it from the aggravated offence, which is considered below.

Actus reus

The actus reus of the simple offence consists of destroying or damaging property belonging to another.

Destroying or damaging

Whether or not something has been damaged is a question of fact and degree and a matter of common sense for the jury or magistrates: *Roe v Kingerlee* (1986).

CHECKPOINT

The courts have held that property has been damaged where *effort and expense* is required to rectify it (*Roe v Kingerlee* 1986), or where the damage has *impaired the usefulness or value* of the property (*Fiak* 2005). The nature and purpose of the property is relevant in this regard, so that a scratch to a scaffolding pole was not damage within the meaning of the 1971 Act in *Morphitis v Salmon* 1990.

The following have been held to amount to "damage": writing graffiti on a concrete pillar with a marker pen (*Blake v DPP* (1993)); spraying paint on to a pavement so that the local authority had to remove it with high-pressure water jets (*Hardman v Chief Constable of Avon & Somerset Constabulary* (1986)); and, applying mud to the wall of a police cell (*Roe v Kingerlee* (1986)). On the other hand, spitting on a policeman's raincoat has been held not to constitute damage because the garment could easily be wiped clean with a damp cloth: *A [a juvenile] v R* (1978).

The Computer Misuse Act 1990 s.3(6) provides that modifying the contents of a computer does not constitute criminal damage to the computer or any computer storage medium unless it impairs its physical condition. Such interference is now caught by offences under the 1990 Act.

Property

Section 10(1) of the 1971 Act provides that property means property of a tangible nature, including land. This differs from the definition given to property in the **Theft Act 1968**.

Belonging to another

Under s.10(2) of the 1971 Act, property belongs to any person having the custody or control of it; having in it any proprietary right or interest; or having a charge on it. This is substantially the same meaning as in the **Theft Act 1968**.

Mens rea

The mens rea for criminal damage is intention or recklessness as to destroying or damaging property belonging to another. Recklessness in this context is subjective: *G* (2003) (see Ch.2). However, D does not have to intend, or foresee a risk, that what he does will be regarded as damage. In *Seray-Wurie v DPP* (2012) D wrote messages on two parking signs with a marker pen. D maintained that his intention was to pass on information and he did not intend to cause damage. The Divisional Court held that D's intention to write on the signs was sufficient to establish the mens rea of simple criminal damage; it was for the magistrates to determine whether the messages constituted damage in law.

Defences

The definition of criminal damage includes the words "without lawful excuse". Any of the general defences available under statute or at common law may provide a lawful excuse. In addition, the 1971 Act provides two specific lawful excuses which are applicable only to criminal damage.

LEGISLATION HIGHLIGHTER

Under s.5(2) of the Act a defendant has a lawful excuse for his actions if:

(a) the defendant honestly believed he had the consent of the relevant person, or would have if that person had known the circumstances; or

(b) he acted as he did in order to protect property that he believed was in immediate need of protection, and he believed the means used were reasonable.

The test of such belief is subjective: provided the belief is honest it does not matter that it was unreasonable. See *Jaggard v Dickinson* (Ch.6). Nevertheless, the subsection is still interpreted strictly.

In *Hunt* (1978) D assisted his wife, who was the warden of a block of flats for the elderly. He set fire to some bedding in order to draw attention to a problem with the fire alarm system. The Court of Appeal dismissed his appeal and held that, given what D honestly believed, the question of whether he acted in order to protect property was an objective test.

KEY CASE

In HILL; HALL (1988) the Ds were anti-nuclear protestors. They travelled to a US naval base in Wales intending to cut the perimeter fence with hacksaws. They argued that the presence of the base would make the area a target if hostilities broke out between America and the Soviet Union and, consequently, the surrounding property was in need of protection. The Court of Appeal held that the defence could not apply because their actions were not capable of protecting property. Furthermore, the property in question was not in immediate need of protection.

SUMMARY OF CRIMINAL DAMAGE

ACTUS REUS
D must:
- destroy or damage property; and
- the property must belong to another.

MENS REA
D must:
- intend to destroy or damage any such property, or
- be subjectively reckless as to destroying or damaging any such property (i.e. property belonging to another).

AGGRAVATED CRIMINAL DAMAGE

Under s.1(2) of the 1971 Act it is an offence intentionally or recklessly to destroy or damage property intending to endanger life thereby or being reckless as to whether life is endangered. This offence is known as aggravated criminal damage and the maximum punishment is life imprisonment.

Actus reus

For the aggravated offence, the actus reus consists of the destruction of, or damage to, property. Note that, unlike the simple offence, the property does not have to belong to another.

Mens rea

In addition to intending or being reckless as to the damage or destruction the defendant must intend to endanger life, or be reckless as to doing so. That requirement is absent if the defendant did not foresee a risk that human life would be endangered. However, it is what is in the defendant's mind that is important and there does not have to be any actual danger to life: *Parker* (1993).

The word "thereby" is significant. The defendant has to have intended or been reckless as to endangering life by the criminal damage or destruction.

KEY CASE

In **STEER (1987)**, D fired a rifle at the window of a house. No injuries were caused to those inside. He pleaded guilty to aggravated criminal damage but then appealed. The House of Lords held that the intention or recklessness envisaged by s.1(2) of the 1971 Act was directed to the possible danger to life caused by the destruction or damage to property. It was not sufficient that D intended or was reckless as to endangering life by shooting. To be guilty under s.1(2) he had to intend or be reckless as to endangering life by the criminal damage (i.e. by the broken glass).

The Court of Appeal followed *Steer* in the cases of *Webster; Warwick* (1995). In the first case, D pushed a heavy stone over a railway bridge onto a passing train. It penetrated the roof and passengers were showered with debris, although none were injured. The Court of Appeal held that D's conviction under s.1(2) could not be justified on the basis that D had intended to endanger life by his act of dropping the stone (e.g. by the stone hitting a passenger). However, it could be justified on the basis that he had been reckless as to whether life would be endangered by the damage to the roof causing material to fall on the passengers. In the second case, D drove a car from which bricks were thrown at a police car, smashing its windows and showering the officers with glass. It was held that liability under s.1(2) depended upon whether D intended or was reckless as to breaking the window and whether he intended or was reckless as to whether any resulting damage would endanger life. The judge had properly directed the jury and the conviction was upheld.

More recently, in *Wenton* (2010), D smashed the window of a house with a brick and then threw a petrol bomb through the broken window. The Court of Appeal quashed D's conviction for aggravated criminal damage on the ground that D had not intended or been reckless as to endangering life by the damage to the window.

It may be that a defendant causes damage different from that which he intended or foresaw. In determining whether the defendant intended to endanger life by the criminal damage (or was reckless as to doing so), one looks not at the criminal damage which he actually caused, but at the criminal damage he intended to cause or was reckless as to causing. Even if the damage actually caused is slight, there can still be liability under s.1(2): *Dudley* (1989).

Defences

The lawful excuses provided by s.5(2) do not apply to aggravated criminal damage, although the defendant remains entitled to rely on any general defence available under statute or at common law.

ARSON

Under s.1(3), if either of the above offences under s.1(1) and 1(2) is committed by fire the offence is one of arson, punishable by a maximum of life imprisonment.

REVISION CHECKLIST

You should now know and understand:

☐ the elements of theft, handling stolen goods, burglary, robbery and blackmail;

☐ the meaning of the term "appropriation";

- the statutory situations in which a person is not dishonest and the test to be applied where none of these situations pertains;
- the timing of the force required for robbery;
- the distinction between the two different types of burglary;
- the meaning of "menaces";
- the elements of simple criminal damage;
- the definition of the term "damage";
- the circumstances in which a defendant may have a "lawful excuse" for simple criminal damage;
- the differences between simple criminal damage and the aggravated form of the offence;
- when a defendant should be charged with arson.

QUESTION AND ANSWER

QUESTION

Gavin's boss, Alexander, owes him some money. One day, Gavin waits until Alexander has gone home and then goes into Alexander's office intending to take some money from the petty cash tin. He opens the petty cash tin but it is empty, so he takes a painting which he estimates is of the same value as the money he is owed. On his way out of the building with the painting he is challenged by Alexander's secretary, Nancy. Gavin pushes Nancy to the ground and runs off.

Discuss Gavin's liability under the **Theft Act 1968**.

ADVICE AND THE ANSWER

You should begin by identifying the various offences that Gavin may have committed, namely theft, burglary and robbery. Because theft is an element of both burglary and robbery, your answer should begin by considering whether Gavin is liable for theft. You should define theft and then consider each element of the offence in turn, before moving on to do the same with the offences of burglary and robbery.

Under Theft Act 1968 s.1, theft is committed if a person dishonestly appropriates property belonging to another, with intent to permanently deprive the other of it. Any assumption of the rights of an owner amounts to appropriation (s.3). By opening the petty cash tin, Gavin has assumed one of the rights of an owner, which is sufficient (*Morris* 1984). He also appropriates the painting when he takes it. Both the petty cash tin and the painting are property and both belong to Alexander.

Gavin does not intend to permanently deprive Alexander of the petty cash tin and a conditional intention to deprive Gavin of its contents is insufficient (*Easom* 1971). However, he clearly does intend to permanently deprive Alexander of the painting. By taking the painting away with him, Gavin has treated it as his own to dispose of regardless of Alexander's rights (s.6).

Is Gavin dishonest? Dishonesty is not defined in the Theft Act, but s.2 sets out three situations in which a person is not dishonest. Alexander owes Gavin some money. If Gavin believes that he has a right in law to take the painting to compensate him for the money he is owed, then he is not dishonest (s.2(1)(a)). He must believe that he has a legal right, rather than a moral right to take the painting for this section to apply. The fact that Gavin waits until Alexander has left for the day perhaps suggests that he does not believe that he has a legal right to take any of Alexander's property. If Gavin does not fall within s.2(1)(a), the *Ghosh* test must be applied. The jury will be directed to consider whether Gavin's actions were dishonest according to the ordinary standards of reasonable and honest people. If they were, the next question is whether Gavin realised that his actions were dishonest by those standards. Again, the fact that Gavin waited until Alexander had gone home suggests that he realised that ordinary people would regard his actions as dishonest. Gavin is, therefore, guilty of theft.

Gavin may also be liable for burglary under both s.9(1)(a) and s.9(1)(b). Both types of burglary require a defendant to have entered a building or part of a building as a trespasser. Gavin enters part of a building when he goes into Alexander's office. Although he may have had a general permission to be in his employer's office, he exceeds that permission (and becomes a trespasser) when he enters intending to steal from the petty cash tin. Presumably he knows that he is exceeding any permission that he may have, because he waits until Alexander has left for the day. He, therefore, has the mens rea required of a trespasser.

Gavin will be guilty of s.9(1)(a) burglary if he intends to commit one of the ulterior offences set out in s.9(2) at the time of entry. Here he intends to steal money and theft is one of the specified offences. It does not matter that he is unable to find any money to steal

(*Walkington* 1979). Gavin is also guilty of s.9(1)(b) burglary because, having entered the office as a trespasser, he actually steals the painting.

Robbery occurs where a defendant uses force, or puts or seeks to put someone in fear of force, immediately before or at the time of stealing and in order to steal. After stealing the painting, Gavin uses force on Nancy. The issue here is whether this can be said to be force used at the time of stealing. It is clear that appropriation can be a continuing act (*Atakpu and Abrahams* 1994). Here Gavin uses force in order to escape, so it is arguable that he is still in the act of stealing when he pushes Nancy to the ground (*Hale* 1979). Gavin may, therefore, be liable for robbery.

Fraud and non-payment

In addition to the **Theft Act 1968,** dishonesty offences can be found in the Theft Act 1978 and the **Fraud Act 2006.** The latter repealed a number of deception offences that were previously contained in the Theft Acts 1968 and 1978. Many of these former offences involved the defendant dishonestly obtaining something (e.g. property, services, a pecuniary advantage, or a money transfer) by deception. The Fraud Act replaced them with new offences, the two principal offences being fraud (s.1) and obtaining services dishonestly (s.11).

FRAUD

LEGISLATION HIGHLIGHTER

Fraud is an offence contrary to s.1 of the **Fraud Act 2006.** Sections 2, 3 and 4 set out the three different ways in which fraud can be committed, namely by false representation (s.2); by failing to comply with a legal duty to disclose information (s.3); or by abuse of position (s.4).

Context

Prior to the **Fraud Act 2006,** there were a number of specific statutory offences that were designed to penalise fraudulent behaviour. These included theft, various deception offences and fraudulent trading. There was also a common law offence of conspiracy to defraud.

The eight statutory deception offences found in the Theft Acts of 1968 and 1978 included obtaining property, services, a pecuniary advantage, and a money transfer, by deception. These offences were criticised by both academics and the judiciary as being too specific. As such, they were unable to capture the wide range of fraudulent behaviour that most people would consider to be criminal. For example, a person who dishonestly obtained a benefit by giving false information to a machine could not be guilty of a deception offence because a machine has no mind and, therefore, cannot be deceived. This became increasingly problematic as businesses made more use of computers and other machines to interact with their customers.

Meanwhile, the common law offence of conspiracy to defraud suffered the opposite problem of being too widely defined. This offence captured any dishonest agreement to make a gain at the expense of another person. As the Law Commission pointed out, "[in] a capitalist society, commercial life revolves around the pursuit of gain for oneself and, as a corollary, others may lose out, whether directly or indirectly" (Law Com No.276, 2002). Thus, the question of whether an offence had been committed depended on the definition of dishonesty, which was determined by the application of the *Ghosh* test (see Ch.10). The first limb of the *Ghosh* test requires consideration of whether a defendant's conduct was dishonest by the ordinary standards of reasonable and honest people. This means that activities become dishonest if a jury decides to categorise them as dishonest. The Law Commission gave the example of the directors of a company engaging in "industrial espionage" to gain an advantage over a competitor. If a jury was prepared to categorise this behaviour as dishonest according to their standards, the directors would potentially be liable for conspiracy to defraud, even though Parliament had never created an offence of industrial espionage.

The Law Commission recommended the creation of a single statutory offence of fraud to simplify the law and to make it fairer. In 2006, Parliament enacted the **Fraud Act 2006**, which was largely based on the Law Commission's recommendations. The Act created a single offence that could be committed in three different ways. The statutory deception offences were all abolished, although conspiracy to defraud at common law remains.

Fraud by false representation—section 2

Section 2 of the 2006 Act provides that a person is liable for fraud if he dishonestly makes a false representation, intending to make a gain for himself or another, or intending to cause loss to another or expose another to a risk of loss.

Actus reus

The actus reus of this form of fraud consists of making a false representation. It can be a representation of fact or law and includes a representation as to a person's state of mind: s.2(3). Section 2(2) provides that a representation is false if it is untrue or misleading. Even if D believes the representation to be false, he will not be liable if the representation is technically true: *Cornelius* (2012). A representation can be express or implied (s.2(4)) and can be made by words or by conduct. For example, according to the explanatory notes to the Act, a person who dishonestly misuses a credit card to pay for something makes a false representation by conduct.

Section 2(5) confirms that the method by which the representation is made is immaterial. Under this subsection a representation is made if it is submitted in any form to any system or device concerned with communications. Thus, a representation made to a machine is covered by the Act. This would include, for example, a person who dishonestly enters someone else's PIN number into a machine, or someone who puts a foreign coin into a vending machine.

Mens rea

There are three mens rea requirements:

(a) the person making the representation must have knowledge that it is, or might be, untrue or misleading;

(b) dishonesty; and

(c) an intention to make a gain or to cause a loss (or risk causing a loss) to another person by making the false representation.

"Dishonesty" is determined using the *Ghosh* test (see Ch.10).

CHECKPOINT

"Gain" and "loss" have similar meanings to those relevant for the offence of blackmail (see Ch.10).

Section 5 of the Fraud Act 2006 states:

"(2) 'Gain' and 'loss'

(a) extend only to gain or loss in money or other property;

(b) include any such gain or loss whether temporary or permanent;

and 'property' means any property whether real or personal (including things in action and other intangible property).

(3) 'Gain' includes a gain by keeping what one has, as well as a gain by getting what one does not have.

(4) 'Loss' includes a loss by not getting what one might get, as well as a loss by parting with what one has."

D must intend to make a gain or cause loss **by the false representation**; a causative link is required between D's intention and the making of the false representation: *Gilbert* (2012). Those caught by this section would include a person who knowingly tells lies when: (i) applying for a job; (ii) applying for insurance; (iii) making an insurance claim; (iv) applying for a mortgage loan or an overdraft; or (v) begging. This offence is also committed by those who engage in "phishing" (i.e. sending e-mails purporting to come from financial institutions, which seek the recipients' account numbers and security information). The offence is committed even if the intended gain (or loss) never actually materialises, e.g. because the person hearing or reading the lie recognises it for what it is.

Fraud by failing to disclose information—section 3

Under s.3, fraud is committed if D dishonestly fails to disclose information to another person which he is under a legal duty to disclose. D must intend to make a gain for himself or another, or to cause loss to another, or to expose another to a risk of loss, by failing to disclose the information.

According to the Law Commission, a legal duty to disclose information:

> "may derive from statute (such as the provisions governing company prospectuses), from the fact that the transaction in question is one of the utmost good faith (such as a contract of insurance), from the express or implied terms of a contract, from the custom of a particular trade or market, or from the existence of a fiduciary relationship between the parties (such as that of agent and principal)." (Law Com No.276, 2002, para.7.28.)

Thus, this section will apply to someone who applies for life insurance and dishonestly fails to disclose that he has had a heart attack. The requirement of utmost good faith in an insurance contract is unusual, however. There is no general duty to disclose information when forming contracts. For example, someone who is offered a picture to buy and recognises it as a Rembrandt is under no duty to disclose that fact to the seller. Buying the picture without making such disclosure will not amount to fraud. Of course, if the buyer told a lie, he might well be guilty of fraud by false representation.

Fraud by abuse of position—section 4

A person commits fraud under s.4 if he occupies a position in which he is expected to safeguard (or not to act against) the financial interests of another person and dishonestly abuses his position. As with the other forms of fraud, he will only be liable if he intends to make a gain for himself or another, or to cause loss to another, or to expose another to a risk of loss, by abusing his position.

Section 4(2) confirms that this offence can be committed by omission as well as by a positive act.

This offence would cover a barman employed in a public house who makes and sells his own sandwiches to customers instead of those supplied by his employer in order to make money for himself. It would also apply to a carer who abused his position by dishonestly persuading his patient to give him money.

In *Gale* (2007) D pleaded guilty to fraud by abuse of position. D was an Office Manager for a courier delivery service based at Heathrow airport. In return for £100 cash, he certified that a crate contained "known cargo". In fact the crate contained khat (which is a drug that is illegal in the USA), although D had no idea what was in it. As a result of D's actions, the crate passed through airport security and then through customs without being screened.

SUMMARY OF FRAUD

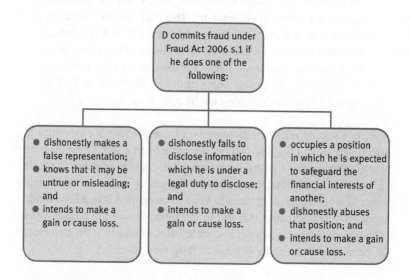

D commits fraud under Fraud Act 2006 s.1 if he does one of the following:

- dishonestly makes a false representation;
- knows that it may be untrue or misleading; and
- intends to make a gain or cause loss.

- dishonestly fails to disclose information which he is under a legal duty to disclose; and
- intends to make a gain or cause loss.

- occupies a position in which he is expected to safeguard the financial interests of another;
- dishonestly abuses that position; and
- intends to make a gain or cause loss.

OBTAINING SERVICES DISHONESTLY

The **Fraud Act 2006** creates an offence of obtaining services by a dishonest act. Under s.11, D will be liable if:

"(1)... he obtains services for himself or another—
   (a) by a dishonest act, and
   (b) in breach of subsection (2).
(2) A person obtains services in breach of this subsection if—
   (a) they are made available on the basis that payment has been, is being or will be made for or in respect of them,

(b) he obtains them without any payment having been made for or in respect of them or without payment having been made in full, and

(c) when he obtains them, he knows—

(i) that they are being made available on the basis described in paragraph (a), or

(ii) that they might be,

but intends that payment will not be made, or will not be made in full."

This offence can only be committed by a positive act. It also requires D to have actually obtained the service in question. The offence would be made out, for example, if D climbed over the wall of a cricket club and watched a cricket match for which an entrance fee was normally payable.

Section 11(2)(a) means that it is not an offence to dishonestly obtain a service which is supplied free of charge. Thus, if D obtains a free service he will not be liable, even if the service would not be free but for his dishonest act. For example, if a non-pensioner obtained free entry to a show by lying and claiming that he was a pensioner, he would not be guilty of an offence under this section. (He might be guilty of fraud by false representation, depending upon whether he intended to make a gain, or to cause a loss or a risk of loss.)

MAKING OFF WITHOUT PAYMENT

Making off without payment is an offence contrary to **Theft Act 1978** s.3(1). If a person knows that payment on the spot is required or expected for goods or services, he commits an offence if he dishonestly makes off without paying, intending to avoid payment.

Context

This offence is required because a defendant who has become the absolute owner of property cannot be liable for theft, the property no longer belonging to another (see Ch.10). For example, in *Edwards v Ddin* (1976), D asked a petrol station attendant to fill his car up with petrol, then dishonestly drove off without paying for it. Under consumer legislation, the property (i.e. the petrol) passed to D when it was put into his car. He was, therefore, not guilty of theft when he subsequently decided not to pay for it. The Criminal Law Revision Committee recommended creating an offence of making off without payment in order to protect legitimate businesses (Thirteenth Report, Cmnd 6733).

Actus reus

The prosecution must prove that payment on the spot was required or expected. If D and V agree that payment can be delayed or deferred, the offence is not committed. This is so even if D obtains an agreement to delay or defer payment by deception: *Vincent* (2001).

The defendant must also make off without paying for the goods or services. In *McDavitt* (1981), D refused to pay for a meal he had consumed in a restaurant. Upon being told that the police had been called, he waited in the toilet for them to arrive. The trial judge directed the jury to acquit D on the ground that he had not made off from the spot where payment was required. Conversely, in *Brooks and Brooks* (1983), D1's conviction for making off without payment from a restaurant was upheld by the Court of Appeal as he had left the premises.

By s.3(3), no offence is committed if the supply of goods or the service is illegal, or if payment would not be legally enforceable.

Mens rea

(i)   The defendant must know that payment on the spot is required or expected;

(ii) he must be dishonest; and

(iii) he must intend to avoid payment. This means an intention to avoid payment permanently. An intention to defer or delay payment is not sufficient: *Allen* (1984).

REVISION CHECKLIST

You should now know and understand:

☐ the reasons that the Fraud Act 2006 was enacted;

☐ the three ways in which fraud can be committed;

☐ the meaning of "false representation";

☐ the circumstances in which a person is under a legal duty to disclose information;

☐ the circumstances in which a person's abuse of his position may lead to liability for fraud;

☐ the definitions of "gain" and "loss";

☐ the elements of the offence of dishonestly obtaining a service;

☐ when a person may be criminally liable for making off without payment.

QUESTION AND ANSWER

QUESTION

Charles is a university student. He drives to lectures from his home and usually pays to park his car in a public car park. One day, as he is leaving his lecture hall, he finds a card on the ground which contains a bar code, the words "University staff car park" and the name "Professor Bluster". He looks around to make sure no one is watching and then pockets the card. The following day Charles uses the card to gain entrance to the staff car park free of charge and parks his car.

Charles has a part-time job on Velocity Trains as a customer service assistant. He believes that Velocity Beer, which is served on board the train, is overpriced. He begins selling his own home brew to passengers at half the price and keeps the money that he makes.

Consider which offences, if any, Charles has committed under the Fraud Act 2006.

ADVICE AND THE ANSWER

Although Charles may also be guilty of theft, note that you are only asked to consider his liability under the **Fraud Act 2006.** You should consider each paragraph of the question in turn. In relation to each, begin by identifying the offence(s) that Charles may have committed.

Staff car park card

Charles may be liable for fraud or for obtaining services dishonestly.

Fraud is committed when a false representation is dishonestly made with the necessary intent (Fraud Act 2006 s.2). The false representation in this case is an implied representation by conduct. By presenting the card to the entrance machine, Charles has falsely represented that he is Professor Bluster. The fact that the representation is made to a machine rather than a person is irrelevant (s.2(5)).

Charles knows that his representation is false. Whether or not he is dishonest is determined using the *Ghosh* test. His actions would surely be regarded as dishonest by the ordinary standards of reasonable and honest people. Furthermore, the fact that Charles looks around before pocketing the card suggests that he realises that his actions are dishonest by ordinary standards. Charles intends to make a gain as he intends to park free of charge in the staff car park. "Gain" includes keeping what one has and Charles will keep the money that he would otherwise have had to pay to park in the public car park. He may also intend to expose Professor Bluster to the risk of loss as Professor Bluster will have to park his car in the public car park until his staff card is replaced.

Alternatively, Charles may be liable for obtaining a service dishonestly (Fraud Act s.11). Charles has obtained a space in the car park, which is a service offered by the University. However, he will only be guilty of this offence if the service requires payment. If the parking space was free, he would not be liable (s.11(2)(a)).

Selling the beer

Charles is liable for fraud by abuse of position (s.4). As an employee, Charles would be expected to safeguard the financial interests of his employer, Velocity Trains. He has abused his position by selling his own produce instead of that of his employers. He keeps the money for himself, which shows that he intends to make a gain for himself. He would also be dishonest applying the *Ghosh* test.

Handy hints

There are two different types of question that arise in criminal law examinations. The first is a problem question, which requires you to consider the facts of a given scenario and consider what possible offences (and potentially defences) arise. The second is an essay question which poses a statement or question on a particular area of criminal law and you are expected to analyse the legal principles and address the statement/question.

Dealing with problem questions

In order to deal with a problem question you should revise the current law relating to each offence. You must know the elements of each offence (actus reus and mens rea) and be able to identify a recent authority to support the current legal position in relation to each element. The key to a good answer for a problem question is the application of the law to the facts given.

Make sure you read through the facts of the scenario carefully. Make a note of the possible offences you have spotted and any defences that may be available. It is important that you always consider offences first – remember there is no need to raise a defence if there is no offence! Next, plan out your answer, by listing the elements of the offence and the facts of the scenario that help prove or disprove each element. In order to make sure that you do not miss any issues, you could use the mnemonic "IDEA":

Identify the possible offence (or defence) arising in the scenario.
Define the offence(or defence) in full, noting each of the elements of the offence (or defence).
Explain, with authority, what each of the elements means in relation to the current state of the law.
Apply the law on each element to the facts of the scenario.

Deal with one offence at a time. You could use the mnemonic for each element of the offence to ensure that you have not missed anything out; identify the element, define the element, explain the law for that element and apply the law to the facts. Then move on to the next element, taking one at a time. It is important to deal with every element of the offence, even if that particular element is very obviously proved, as this will demonstrate your knowledge and understanding of the law. Conclude with whether you think there is liability for that offence before moving on to the next offence. If you are considering an offence which has a separate offence as one of its elements (e.g. theft is a requirement for the offence of robbery), deal with the lesser offence first (e.g. deal with theft in full before considering the remaining requirements for robbery).

Deal with any defences in exactly the same way: identify the defence, define it in full, noting what has to be proved/disproved, explain the law for each element and how the law applies to the facts. Only deal with a defence after considering the offence—there is no need for a defence if no offence can be proved.

TOP TIPS FOR PROBLEM QUESTIONS

- Do get straight to the point
- Do use relevant authority
- Do state the obvious—cover all the elements
- Do discuss both sides of argument if there is no obvious answer
- Do explain your reasoning (credit for "working out")
- Don't repeat the facts of your case authorities in detail—only state what is necessary
- Don't give detailed analysis of existing case law (unless necessary to illustrate a point)
- Don't deal with irrelevant legal points

Dealing with essay questions

In order to prepare for an essay question, you need to understand how the law has developed over the years and what reform proposals have been circulated. You need to form some opinions on the law and on the reforms proposed. It is important that you undertake further reading and research in order to fare well in an essay question as credit will be given where you can support your argument with the views of academic writers, for example. Make use of your textbook to direct you to journal articles or specialist texts on particular areas of the law and try to make a note of some key quotes or viewpoints from academic writers in order that you can use these in an essay. When you see the question, read through it once or twice to ensure you understand what it means. Firstly, find the specific legal topic you are being asking to consider in your answer and make a note of this. Next, try to identify the particular issue which the question is asking you to comment on. Where you are asked to "discuss" an issue in relation to a topic of law, it is often helpful to turn the question into one that has the answer of either "yes" or "no" as this will help you to consider both sides of the argument.

For example:

"The concept of dishonesty in theft is confusing and should be defined in statute in order to ensure that juries are consistent in reaching their verdicts. Discuss."

Here the topic of law to be addressed is dishonesty in the offence of theft. The question is querying whether dishonesty is (1) confusing and, (2) should be defined. If you turn this into a yes/no style question, it would look like this:

Is the concept of dishonesty in theft confusing? Should the concept of dishonesty in theft be defined?

Both of the above questions can be answered with "yes" or "no" and this will help you think of arguments supporting both sides of a "discussion". These arguments will form the basis of the structure of your answer.

The key to a good answer in an essay question is structure. You will only achieve a good structure if you carefully analyse the question (as noted above) and take some time to plan your essay before you start to write the answer. Remember, if you spend a few minutes thinking about the answer, writing your thoughts on rough paper and then ordering your thoughts, you will have the rest of your time to simply write. All your thinking (the time-consuming part) will be done. It is also very important when you are planning your answer, that you remember to always address the question or the statement posed and that you demonstrate an ability to analyse the law (i.e. consider the issue from various points of view).

The basic structure of an essay is as follows:

Introduction
This will usually consist of a single paragraph. Identify the legal issue to be addressed in the question (you will find this by reading the question carefully) and ensure that you define that principle and/or explain the principle in full. You should also indicate the main areas that you intend to discuss (you will know this from analysing what the question is asking you to consider and from planning your essay).

Main body of essay
This is the bulk of the essay which answers the question. You must ensure that you develop the key points outlined in your essay plan. Use one or two paragraphs to develop each point you wish to raise. The paragraphs (points) must flow in a logical order and you must link one paragraph (point) to the

next. Use linking words such as "however", "yet" and "on the other hand". Avoid very long or very short paragraphs and ensure that you do not pass off other people's ideas as your own (plagiarism).

Paragraphs

Start each paragraph with a sentence that expresses the point you want to make. If you can link your point to the title of the essay, this will help to ensure that you are addressing the question. Try to use some authority to support the point you are trying to make and comment on how the authority/ evidence supports your point. Try to explain the implications or con- sequences of your point and conclude the paragraph by linking back to the question again. Ensure that you start your next paragraph by linking to the last one.

Conclusion

Use one final paragraph to conclude your essay. Summarise the main ideas from the body of the essay and give an overall conclusion which relates back to the original question. There is no need to plan your conclusion as it will flow once you have written the rest of your answer.

TOP TIPS FOR ESSAY QUESTIONS

- Revise areas of the law where there has been considerable development or debate
- Ensure you are familiar with the facts of relevant cases as you may have to discuss the facts in an essay question
- Plan your essay before you start to write it out
- Ensure you are answering the question
- Remember to structure your essay
- Try to analyse the law and use authority to support your point of view where possible

---

EXAMINATION REVISION CHECKLIST

CHAPTER 1: ACTUS REUS

(1)   Define the term actus reus.

(2)   Identify three offences that can be committed by omission.

(3)   Identify three situations where D may be under a duty to act.

(4)   Explain the factual test for causation.

(5)   Explain, with reference to at least two authorities, the full legal test for causation.

CHAPTER 2: MENS REA

(1) Define the term mens rea.

(2) Explain, with reference to authority, the concepts of direct and oblique intent.

(3) Explain the concept of subjective recklessness.

(4) What is the effect of the doctrine of transferred malice?

CHAPTER 3: STRICT LIABILITY

(1) What are strict liability offences?

(2) Explain the *Gammon* criteria for determining whether an offence is one of strict liability.

(3) Give three examples of strict liability offences.

(4) Identify two arguments for and against the existence of strict liability offences.

CHAPTER 4: MULTIPLE PARTIES TO A CRIME

(1) Explain the following terms with reference to authority:
   — Aid
   — Abet
   — Counsel
   — Procure

(2) What is required in order to establish a joint enterprise?

(3) Can secondary liability exist where the principal offender has not committed the actus reus of the offence?

(4) Can secondary liability exist where the principal offender has committed the actus reus of the offence but does not possess the requisite mens rea?

(5) Is it possible to withdraw from a joint enterprise?

CHAPTER 5: INCHOATE OFFENCES

(1) Define a criminal attempt.

(2) Can a defendant be guilty of attempting to commit an impossible crime?

(3) Explain the concept of conspiracy.

(4)   What is required to be guilty of encouraging or assisting a criminal offence?

(5)   What defence is available to a charge of encouraging or assisting a crime?

CHAPTER 6: DEFENCES

(1)   Who bears the burden of proving the defence of insanity and what is the required standard of proof?

(2)   What is a "defect of reason" for the purposes of the defence of insanity?

(3)   What is the difference between the defences of automatism and insanity? Give three examples of situations where each of the defences would apply.

(4)   What is a crime of specific intent? What is a crime of basic intent?

(5)   What is the effect of pleading the defence of intoxication to offences of basic and specific intent?

(6)   With reference to authority, explain when use of force (for the purposes of self-defence) will be necessary and reasonable.

(7)   Explain the defence of duress of circumstances.

(8)   Will the defence of duress be available to a defendant who voluntarily joined a criminal gang?

(9)   Explain the distinction between the defence of duress and the defence of necessity.

CHAPTER 7: NON-FATAL OFFENCES AGAINST THE PERSON

(1)   What is a common assault?

(2)   Give three examples of situations where it is possible to consent to harm.

(3)   Define the terms "occasioning" and "actual bodily harm".

(4)   What is the mens rea required for the offence of assault occasioning actual bodily harm under s.47 of the **Offences Against the Person Act 1861**?

(5)   Explain the distinction between section 18 and 20 of the **Offences Against the Person Act 1861**.

(6)   What is a wound?

CHAPTER 8: SEXUAL OFFENCES

(1)   Define the offences of rape, assault by penetration and sexual assault.

(2)   How is the term "sexual" defined by the s.78 of the **Sexual Offences Act 2003**?

(3)   How is consent defined by s.74 of the **Sexual Offences Act 2003**?

(4)   Give three examples of situations in which evidential presumptions about consent will arise under s.75 of the **Sexual Offences Act 2003**.

CHAPTER 9: HOMICIDE

(1)   Explain the elements of the offence of murder.

(2)   Explain the two qualifying triggers, either of which will be required for the partial defence of loss of control.

(3)   In the defence of diminished responsibility, what must the abnormality of mental functioning substantially impair?

(4)   Explain the *Church* test to establish dangerousness in the context of constructive manslaughter.

(5)   What is the required mens rea for the offence of constructive manslaughter?

(6)   With reference to authority, give three examples of when a duty of care will be imposed on the defendant in the context of gross negligence manslaughter.

(7)   Define the term "gross negligence".

CHAPTER 10: OFFENCES AGAINST PROPERTY

(1)   With reference to authorities, explain the term "appropriation".

(2)   Explain the *Ghosh* test for dishonesty.

(3)   Explain, with reference to authority what constitutes an "intention to permanently deprive".

(4)   In addition to theft, what elements are required to be guilty of the offence of robbery?

(5)   What is the material difference between the offence of burglary under s.9(1)(a) and s.9(1)(b) of the **Theft Act 1968**?

(6)   What constitutes "damage" for the purposes of the **Criminal Damage Act 1971**?

(7)   Explain the defence of lawful excuse to a charge of criminal damage.

(8)   What additional elements are required to "aggravate" a charge of criminal damage?

(9)   What is arson?

CHAPTER 11: FRAUD AND NON-PAYMENT

(1)   Explain in what ways it is possible to commit fraud under the **Fraud Act 2006 s.1.**

(2)   What must the prosecution prove in order to establish the actus reus of the offence of making off without payment?

(3)   Is the offence of dishonestly obtaining services made out when the service in question is supplied free of charge?

Index